M000238756

© 2008 Crescent Hill Books, LLC.

All rights reserved. No part of this book may be reproduced in any form without written permission
of the copyright owners. All images in this book have been reproduced with the knowledge and prior
consent of the artists concerned, and no responsibility is accepted by producer, publisher, or printer
for any infringement of copyright or otherwise, arising from the contents of this publication. Every
effort has been made to ensure that credits accurately comply with information supplied. We apologize
for any inaccuracies that may have occurred and will resolve inaccurate or missing information in a
subsequent reprinting of the book.

First published in the United States of America by
Rockport Publishers, a member of
Quayside Publishing Group
100 Cummings Center, Suite 406-L
Beverly, MA 01915
Telephone: (978) 282-9590
Fax: (978) 283-2742
www.rockpub.com

ISBN-13: 978-1-59253-427-2
ISBN-10: 1-59253-427-9

10 9 8 7 6 5 4 3 2 1

Design: John Lee Studio, www.johnleestudio.com
Produced by Crescent Hill Books, Louisville, KY

Printed in China

REALLY GOOD LOGOS
explained

Top Design Professionals Critique 500 Logos & Explain What Makes Them Work

BEVERLY MASSACHUSETTS

ROCKPORT PUBLISHERS

● ● ● **By Margo Chase**
Rian Hughes
Ron Miriello
Alex W. White

CONTENTS

Margo Chase

The Mistakes of Others

"You must learn from the mistakes of others. You can't possibly live long enough to make them all yourself." – Sam Levenson

There are thousands of books about logos—so many that you might wonder why we need another. Most show pretty logos, credit the designer, praise the client, and sometimes even discuss the process. But this book is unique.

The logos in this book are not special because they are particularly beautiful or well designed, although some of them are. These logos are special because they were designed by exceptional designers who were willing to submit their work for public criticism; designers willing to learn from their mistakes; designers willing to try and fail while the rest of us watch safely from the sidelines; designers who are, well . . . brave.

The designers who submitted logos to this book have allowed us to examine, discuss, pick apart and evaluate their work, and publish the results here for all to see. And that is what makes this logo book special. The readers don't just get to see a good logo; they get to read about what makes it good and what could have been improved. The critiques are mini-lessons on good type design with a little typographic history thrown in.

As critics, we have done our best to praise what works and constructively explain what doesn't. Some of the mistakes are obvious, some are amusing, and a few left me at a loss for words. But while there is often room for improvement, there are many smart, witty, and just plain beautiful logos in this collection.

Another enlightening aspect of this book is that we critics often disagree. While, of course, I am generally certain that my opinion is the right one, our disagreement should make it clear that even so-called "experts" can make mistakes. Reading through the comments, I noticed places where something I disliked was ably defended by someone else. And there were other places where someone pointed out errors I had completely missed. We all have plenty left to learn.

Whether you are a designer, a client, or even a critic, there is something to learn from this book. So enjoy the carnage, and then be brave—go make some mistakes of your own.

"There are thousands of books about logos. But this book is unique."

🗨 MC Q & A with Margo Chase

My favorite logos inside this book are
the AA Dove (page 132), Water Exhibit (page 240), and Charity Ride (page 34) logos, for three entirely different reasons. The wooden bird flying away with broken strings trailing behind it is powerful conceptually. The symbolism of cutting the strings is inspiring, and the naive quality of the wooden bird illustration is both poignant and fun. It's the perfect message for a life coach.

I also love the Water Exhibit logo for its elegant restraint. The almost-industrial type is beautifully balanced and integrated into the calligraphic flow of the ink/water.

Hand lettering is something I can't live without, so I have to include the Charity Ride logo with its fabulous fat, Blackletter-inspired letters and tattoo decorations on my list of favorites. It looks like it was fun to design and probably inspired the bikers who participated.

You know your logo is Really Good when
someone who knows NOTHING about design says they love it and someone whose opinion you respect agrees. A great logo should be as loved by designers as it is by non-designers. You know it works when non-designers remember it and want it as a tattoo.

What's the best thing a client ever said to you?
"Wow! You designed that?" It usually goes downhill from there.

What is the worst?
"We want a Nike swoosh."

Or even worse, NOTHING. Hearing nothing is really the worst. It usually means they're not happy and afraid to say so. Whoever said "bad new travels fast" never worked in a creative field. We hardly ever hear bad news straight up. We always have to wait around, imagining the worst, until, weeks later we find out what they were afraid to tell us.

For creative inspiration, I
Fly upside down. Ski. Read. Travel. Shop. Eat. Go to museums.

The smartest thing I ever heard anyone say about logo design is...
"People think that design is styling. Design is not style. It's not about giving shape to the shell and not giving a damn about the guts. Good design is a renaissance attitude that combines technology, cognitive science, human need, and beauty to produce something that the world didn't know it was missing."

— Paola Antonelli

"Ugliness does not sell."

— Raymond Loewy

The best career advice I ever received was...
Work to live, don't live to work. Early in my career I didn't believe it. It took me twenty years to realize that you've got to pick your battles. I think I'm much better at my job now because I have more experience and more perspective. I'm not willing to fall on my sword over every job—only the ones that really matter.

Margo Chase drew her first logos more than 20 years ago for unknown bands that mostly stayed unknown. She believes in rapid, tireless iteration and not moving to the computer until a direction is well formed. Chase Design Group, which is located in Los Angeles, provides research, brand strategy, and identity work for the Fortune 500, among others. Outside of the office, Margo competes flying airplane aerobatics, is an expert alpine skier, and routinely injures herself trying other sports.

10 Mistakes Designers Make When Creating a Logo

By Margo Chase

1. **Designing for yourself.**
   It is crucial to understand for whom a logo is really created. Often the designers and the true audiences for their work have very little in common. Get as much information as you can about who the audience really is. Meet them and talk to them if possible. Then design for them, not for yourself.

2. **Starting with a bad font, not altering a good one, or ignoring letterspacing and weight.**
   All of this falls under the heading of "craft." In the era of the computer, craft gets way too little attention. There are millions of fonts available to every designer; some are wonderful, but most are not. Learn to tell the difference. Most typefaces are created for setting text on pages and in paragraphs and sentences. Logos have a totally different level of scale and emotional impact. The usually small number of letters in a logo will be blown up and closely visible.
   At a minimum, every typeface has spacing issues that need to be addressed by altering the letters for a logotype to work well.

   If you are going to start from an existing font, choose one with letterforms that work visually and conceptually for the words you are using. Then learn to adjust forms and weights to make them work together. The best is to swallow your gum and start adjusting and redrawing the letters where necessary—I use lots of tracing paper—until the shapes start to have the relationships for which I am looking. Then I work to make the weights and spacing harmonious. In a good logo the adjustments shouldn't stand out from the rest of the letters; they should look as if they are equally part of the font.

3. **Not doing your homework/research.**
   It is impossible to design a great logo when you don't know what you are trying to accomplish or what style not to use because a competitor has used it. Do your best to understand the context of the business; who the competition is; what, how, and where the logo will appear; why it is needed and who will see it. Don't expect to get all of your information from the client. Clients often don't understand how design can help them, so they don't provide the right kinds of information. A little digging can go a long way. The more information you have, the more successful your design can be.

4. **Not having a sound strategic case for the design direction.**
   When a designer lacks a sound strategy behind his design, it becomes impossible to defend it against a client's personal taste or prejudices. If all you can say is, "I like it, and I know best because I'm a designer," you are doomed.

5. **Overestimating the client's ability to translate words into visual language.**
   Make sure that you and your client are speaking the same language. It is easy to miss with a logo presentation because the client was expecting something completely different based on your verbal description or their own. When you say "fresh and modern" make sure your client knows what that looks like before you start designing. When the client speaks those words, they may have something quite different in mind than you do. Show pictures and get reactions. Find out if their idea of modern is 1957 or 2007.

6. **Not considering the limitations of reproduction.**
   This is a classic error, usually stemming from inexperience, lack of technical understanding, or just not asking enough questions. Find out how the logo will be used before you start designing. Nothing is worse than selling your client on a logo that looks great in full color detail, and then finding out that it will only be printed in silk screen or embroidered.

7. **Not considering other points of view.**
   There are many humorous examples of designs with connotations that were never intended. Perhaps the most notorious is the too-tight spacing between the "L" and "I" in "MEGAFLICKS." Or did the people who named the company "Who Represents?" or "Experts Exchange" think about how their URLs would read? Pay attention to other ways that your work can be interpreted. This is especially true if you are designing something that will be translated into another language. To see some funny examples, do an Internet search on "bad logos."

8. **Using computer tricks.**
   This usually results from trying to decorate a weak design. Applications like Illustrator, Photoshop, and Painter can be a huge asset to any designer, but they should be used with restraint. A bad logotype that is warped, beveled, and drop-shadowed is still a bad logotype. A good one would be better off without that stuff. Generally, if you are thinking of using a computer trick, go lie down until the feeling goes away.

9. **Being a slave to the computer and forgetting to use your fingers.**
   Logos and lettering were created by hand for hundreds of years, and there are many effects and techniques that cannot be replicated digitally. Distressed textures, calligraphy in endless styles, free-flowing scripts, and happy accidents are impossible to create believably using only the computer. Even the best CGI metal effect using deboss (debossing?) filters and good shadows misses the beauty of the same thing modeled in real metal. Computer effects can be great tools for creating a comp that you can sell to the client, but don't rely on them. If the logo needs to look handmade, make it by hand!

10. **Presenting a design you don't want chosen.**
    If you have a few designs to present, and you really don't like one, don't include it to fill out the presentation. It WILL get chosen.

Rian Hughes

Navigating Designland

Good logos require good clients, not just good designers.

If you've just bought (or you're thinking about buying) this book, you're probably either a graphic designer or someone who uses the skills of a graphic designer—a graphic designer's client. The advice set out in this book is intended to guide the critical analysis of what does and does not make a logo a "Really Good Logo" (and not just an "all right, I suppose" logo). The advice in this book is relevant for clients just as much as it is for designers.

The client's role in the design process is crucial. How can clients ensure they get the best from their designers? How can they get the most creative and appropriate logos possible?

With all the talented designers that graduate every year, we should be surrounded by beautiful and original designs. There should be no space left for the mediocre, the plain ugly. Yet it's still out there—on billboards, in supermarkets, on shop fasciae.

Why? Bad designers? Sure, but I hazard that there may be another reason: there are clients who don't know bad from good, who are, in effect, visually tone-deaf. This book will help those clients become more critically informed, to know when they are working with good designers rather than jobbing amateurs or BS merchants who hide behind a smokescreen of mystifying terminology. In addition, this book will help clients as well as designers appreciate, and more important, articulate what separates good design from bad.

Sure, some differences in opinion may be attributed to that elusive thing called "taste." But if a logo has an original concept, is well designed, and is appropriate for its intended use, then the informed client, regardless of his appreciation of aesthetics, will reap the benefits. The informed client will present the designer with a well thought out brief so the designer will know when his solution fulfills the client's needs and when he's way off beam. The informed client will expect originality and not ask the designer to clone the look of the competition. The informed client will know when something is beautiful or ugly and expect the designer to know *why*. The informed client will not be too prescriptive (there's no point in having a dog and barking yourself) but will offer reasoned feedback so the designer can arrive at the final logo with ease. Most of all, good design relies on a clear dialogue between client and designer.

It may sometimes seem as if designers and clients speak entirely different languages, but this book will help you navigate "designland" without accidentally ordering a dog's dinner.

> "There are clients who don't know bad from good, who are, in effect, visually tone-deaf. This book will help those clients."

Q & A with Rian Hughes

My favorite logos inside this book are
the Lab series (pages 28–29) and Voiceover Artist (page 260).
Both have strong concepts and are elegantly executed with no
extraneous fuss.

You know your logo is "Really Good" when
it stands the test of time and is still in use and still looking good ten years
down the line.

What's the best thing a client ever said to you?
"We knew it was right the moment we saw it. We love it. We're not changing
anything."

What is the worst?
"Can you do it again but use this freeware font?" (It was a font based on Iron
Maiden's logo.)

or…

(pointing to an area of negative space) "Did something fall off
the artwork here?"

or…

"We ran out of time so we handed your roughs to our in-house designer to
see what he could do with them. It's just gone to press."

For creative inspiration, I
immerse myself in all aspects of the project, then sleep on it.

**The smartest thing I ever heard anyone say about logo
design is…**
"Design a good logo and people will respond to it like a cool clothing
label—they'll wear it on T-shirts, carry a bag with it on it, feel part of the
brand—all of which adds up to free advertising."

The best career advice I ever received was…
"Ideas never go out of fashion." (Brian Grimwood)

Rian Hughes (devicefonts.co.uk), award-winning graphic
designer, comic artist, and typographer, has produced designs
for watches, CDs, animated films, and Hawaiian shirts for
clients from Tokyo to New York. He has a cabinet of
Thunderbirds memorabilia, a fridge full of vodka, and a stack
of easy listening albums that he plays very quietly.

CHRIS ENRIGHT | VOICEOVER ARTIST

10 Mistakes Designers Make When Creating a Logo

By Rian Hughes

1. **The designer didn't have an idea.**
Moving random fonts around until the arrangement looks nice is not having an idea. Lining up the ascenders and descenders is not having an idea. Taking the initials of the client and combining them into a monogram is an idea, but just barely. Stop and ask yourself a few questions: What is the purpose of this logo? What adjectives would you use to describe the product/company? What image does the logo need to concisely convey? Where will it be used, and how? To what audience are you speaking? How can you address all the above in a memorable and original way? Just considering these questions should give you a handful of good ideas.

2. **The designer had an idea, but it was a bit cliché.**
Clichés sometimes lead somewhere more interesting so, by all means, explore them. But making the letter "O" into a smiling face? I think we've seen that before. As it helps to have an idea or ten before you start, think before you do. Doodle before you Mac.

3. **The designer had an idea, but it wasn't appropriate.**
Your lovingly crafted grunge/skate logo doesn't look right on a pack of fondant fancies? Read that brief again, and apply yourself to the job at hand, even if you desperately wish you were doing rap album sleeves instead.

4. **The designer had a lame idea and tried to dress it up to make it look more impressive.**
Use your Photoshop drop shadows, embossing effects, and filters with caution. They can add a final sheen, but a drop shadow is not a replacement for an idea.

5. **The client didn't understand the designer's idea.**
It helps if your idea is so strong as to be unarguable. However, since some clients may be visually tone-deaf, a short paragraph explaining what the concept is and why it's appropriate often helps.

6. **The design was conceptually or technically inconsistent.**
If the logo is two different ideas combined, it'll probably communicate neither idea effectively. Try not to indulge the client's request to "combine this logo with a bit of that logo" because that is like bolting a rear spoiler on your Model T. Also, remember that the byline is part of the logo too and should adhere to the same overall concept.

Spotting technical inconsistencies is the visual equivalent of hearing a bum note in an orchestra. The curves should be well drawn, the line weights consistent, the underlying grid adhered to, the colors appropriate and harmonious. The white space should be considered. The type choices and sizes should be appropriate and relate elegantly. This is the part where the designer usually knows far more than the client, which is why discussions about kerning can feel like talking poetry to the taxman. It's usually best to sell a client a logo design using arguments based on concepts (see Mistake Number 5), as they're easier to communicate.

7. **The designer let the client have too much input.**
The best designers know how to politely let the client know when he has suggested a lame idea. Then you offer him a much better one. That's your job. (Here it helps to be a master politician; try to charm and persuade rather than pout and cry.)

8. **The design looked just like another design that was already out there.**
Be original. Originality means creating something new, not lifting from an obscure source on the Web, this book, or the chap sitting opposite you in the studio. Use your own voice.

Marketing departments, who find novelty unsettling and ride fashions rather than set them, will here be your occasional nemesis. Dealing with them is a careful dance. Learn to step nimbly and lead with a light hand. Originality and sales are not mutually exclusive. Also see Mistake Number 1, "not having a good idea."

9. **The design wasn't versatile, so the client felt obliged to make "adjustments" in use.**
Think of the applications. A logo doesn't exist in isolation. If it's likely to appear on a shop fascia, it needs to be long and thin. If there are going to be carrier bags, then a squarer version, possibly with stacked type, may work best. Is it going to be used on a busy background? Then an outline or a box may be a good idea. Sometimes logos are supplied in multiple versions: color, web-safe color, black and white, portrait, landscape. It's best to supply a suite of perfectly finessed and related logos than to risk seeing the mess the in-house design department made when trying to adapt your logo to fit on the side of the company jet.

10. **The designer forgot to invoice.**
I can't help you with this one. Give yourself a slap on the forehead.

Ron Miriello

The Aesthetics of the Left Brain

What I have grown to enjoy most about my work as a designer is how it demands that I keep my thinking elastic and pliable, and how it promotes both right- and left-brain thinking at the same time.

In my experience, most clients are very uncomfortable in a discussion of aesthetics. Very squishy stuff, aesthetics. It's the kind of thing that is hard to present to "the board" or measure in the P&L or justify as a line item. But the best designers are also effective communicators who don't force aesthetics. Rather, they begin with a real curiosity to understand the "left-brain" business objectives first—objectives like, "We're losing our market edge to those guys from Zizzerpicker," or "We make superior products that not enough people know about," or "I don't think our customers know what we're passionate about in here."

The best designers are very good at figuring out the problem they're going to solve. And, very often, it's not the problem they're told it is. (I wouldn't think much of a doctor who believed my own diagnosis for stomach pains.) Often the right brain serves as the visionary that diagnoses the problem after the left brain has first explored its parameters.

Aesthetics is "the artistry and inventiveness brought to the problem solving after it is well understood by the left brain." When the left and right brains work together to grapple with a design problem, great things can come about. If the right or the left brain get too heavy-handed, things can get out of whack in a hurry.

There are no rules for how design must be done. After all, it is the opportunity for personal expression that attracts people to the design profession. But there is a discipline to how the design process can work best for our clients and still create award-winning, timeless design. And this book can be a good tool to better understand what goes on in the minds of the designers who have made peace with their roles as highly inventive left-brain, right-brain thinkers. I certainly found it to be an inspiration. I hope you will, too.

"The best designers are also effective communicators."

15

RM Q & A with Ron Miriello

My favorite logo inside this book is...
The St. David's Academy logo (page 151). This is a perfect solution for the client, a rugby academy in England. Rugby is a rough sport, and the logo needed to communicate that. This one succeeds on many levels.

You know your logo is "Really Good" when
every time you see it, you think, "I'm glad I'm the one who came up with that!"

What's the best thing a client ever said to you?
"You're not just designing graphics and products, are you? You're actually designing your life."

What is the worst?
When the first words out of the client's mouth starts with "That logo reminds me a little of ..."

For creative inspiration, I
discipline myself to create as many ideas as quickly as I can in my journal book. The exercise is not to judge them or go back and evaluate them yet, but rather to create a volume of exploration first and avoid falling in love with anything too soon.

The smartest thing I ever heard anyone say about logo design is...
"It's not about what the logo says to me that's important. It's about what it says to my customers."
　　　　　　　—A wise and selfless client from the past

The best career advice I ever received was...
"The good designers are the ones working at their desks. They're not the ones down at the cafés talking about design. Design requires discipline and diligence."
　　　　　　　—John Sorbie, my college graphics professor

Most designers probably don't know that
some of the best directions can come from your clients. Consider them valuable partners who know their business in ways you never will. (On the other hand, there are many times you'll need to save them from themselves.)

ST DAVID'S
ACADEMY

Ron Miriello is principal of Miriello Grafico (miriellografico.com), a San Diego–based design firm whose clients include Sprint PCS, FedEx Kinkos, and Nissan. His Italian roots often call him home to Italy. And his insatiable curiosity toward life often leads him to unique places, including junkyards and international flea markets, where he enjoys finding items to reshape into new designs.

10 Mistakes Designers Make When Creating a Logo

By Ron Miriello

1. **Not understanding the desired brand position.**
   What is the company or brand trying to express? Always design with that answer at the top of your mind.

2. **Starting the design process without a clear objective.**
   Using creative development to lead business decision making can be a recipe for failure. It is often experimental, time-consuming, and expensive for both you and your client.

3. **Creating a design that doesn't work in the applications required.**
   I wish I knew the design had to work on a tie tack! I never would have designed with such detail. Know ahead of time the variety of applications planned and their limitations.

4. **Falling in love with a design you've created too early.**
   Doing so kills objectivity and the potential for even better solutions. Fight the urge to push back too soon.

5. **Fine-tuning solutions early on in the process.**
   Challenge yourself to generate numerous ideas in a fixed amount of time. Most problems are solved in quick sketch form, yet most time is invested in computerized refinements.

6. **Disregarding direction because of its source.**
   All feedback is valuable. Welcome it and encourage it throughout the process. (You may even be handed a jewel to polish.)

7. **Being afraid to speak up.**
   Say you're asked for an "honest opinion," and you know the answer will be hard for your client to swallow. If you have a viewpoint, share it respectfully. Having the courage to express yourself positively in difficult situations is a virtue.

8. **Using the client's money to pay for a style that you love.**
   Don't jam a style into a design because you happen to think it's cool. Be disciplined. Does it help the communication objective? Will it endure after that style has passed?

9. **Showing too many versions.**
   Drive and streamline the process by showing a minimum number of your best, most appropriate solutions. Depending on the project, present no more than four to seven preliminary designs in Phase One.

10. **Not being able to answer the question "Why?"**
    If your answer to an inquiry about your design solution is, "I like the typeface," or "The colors work well together," then you shouldn't be accepting money for your work.

Alex W. White

A Nonstop Discussion of Design

A logo is a business suit. It is the way a business dresses itself. Individuality and expressive meaning are necessary. A logo's excellence represents a business's quality and integrity. A logo is also a microcosm of graphic design: there are a limited number of relationships that must be resolved in a way that looks thoughtful and purposeful. A logo must balance contrasts to make the mark visible, and similarities to give it design unity.

As in any other design solution, it is not enough to merely have nothing wrong with a logo. There must be something demonstrably right with a logo. The opposite of "really good" is not "bad," "mediocre," or even "dreadful." The opposite of "really good" is "random."

There are five considerations to making a design artful:
1) A great idea, simplified to its essence
2) Knowledgeable management of content
3) Precise relationships
4) Exact spacing
5) Elegant execution

So, what is right with any given mark in this book? If a sample includes hand lettering, what makes it good hand lettering or just some stuff? What makes its spacing right? Or its use of rules? What specifically keeps a logo from being just a collection of pieces that have nothing to do with one another?

What makes this book different from other logo books is our comments, which help you understand what makes the logos work—and sometimes what would make them work even better. Most books just show you samples and leave it to you to figure out what makes them good—or just swipe the designs as your own. This book is a tool that, when used properly, illustrates how to see critically by accurately deconstructing a design and gives you the understanding to construct your own really good logos. Better than that, it is a nonstop discussion of design contrasts and relationships that you can apply to any design process, not just to logo design.

"The opposite of 'really good' is not 'bad,' 'mediocre,' or even 'dreadful.' The opposite of 'really good' is 'random.' "

19

Q & A with Alex W. White

My favorite logo inside this book is...
While many logos in this book use negative space as a positive shape with great skill, Impande (page 100) is an outstanding balance between concept and execution. It is superior corporate clothing that thoroughly avoids random design relationships.

You know your logo is "Really Good" when...
it uses negative space, or ground, as effectively as it uses figures.

What's the best thing a client ever said to you?
"Please do another project for us."

What is the worst?
"We're moving in another direction."

For creative inspiration, I
look at centuries-old typography and fine art for relationships I can reinterpret.

The smartest thing I ever heard anyone say about logo design is...
"Simplify."

The best career advice I ever received was...
"In the process of satisfying the job brief, do it the way you think it needs to be done."

Most designers probably don't know that
of the three design elements, type, image, and space, type handling has by far the greatest potential to improve a project. Absorbing type's rules and becoming sensitive to relationships between type and space make the most profound impact on design.

Alex W. White is an advertising and editorial design consultant and the author of five books, including *Advertising Design and Typography* and *The Elements of Graphic Design.* He is the president of the Type Directors Club and has taught for twenty-five years, currently as a visiting professor at Parsons School of Design in New York. He lives in Connecticut and watches deer and coyotes from his office, which is lined with barn siding, a heck of a sound system, and a wall of repurposed taxidermy.

10 Mistakes Designers Make When Creating a Logo

By Alex W. White

1. **Not pairing abstraction to the scale of the business.**
   A local plumbing service needs greater specificity than a regional plumbing supply company, and a national plumbing manufacturer can have still more abstraction.

2. **Attending only to figure and not to ground.**
   Logos are such finite gems that every part must be considered and fully used.

3. **Designing a logo in a vacuum.**
   Always collect competitors' logos and design to exceed that specific universe. Present these logos before showing your studies. This provides context and allows your solution to appear superior to others with whom your client will be compared.

4. **Neglecting to blend at least two distinctive ideas together for fresh results.**
   "Barbecue" plus "Iceland" are far more useful together than alone as descriptors of an Icelandic restaurant.

5. **Not matching the logo with the character of the business.**
   The more specific the business, the more expressive the logo design should be. The more global the business, the more abstract the logo should be.

6. **Not giving the logo enough distinction from its competitors.**
   Neutral is forgettable. Quirky—in a way that promotes character—is memorable.

7. **Not investing time to understand the clients' unique standing in the business community.**
   What makes them viable, and how can those qualities be expressed symbolically?

8. **Using the same pieces as everyone else.**
   The fonts and treatments on your computer are like frozen food: mix them any way you like, but there is a definite limit to how distinctive your cooking can be. Instead, craft materials off computer and then import them.

9. **The designer neglects to optimize the logo for color, gray scale, and line art reproduction.**
   Or the designer neglects to provide basic guidelines for the logo's use.

10. **The designer does not prepare scalable artwork that would ensure all type and spacing remain consistently the same.**

"Buying creative work is hard. Remember this the next time your work is on the table. Help your client by offering rational reasons to support what is essentially an emotional decision."

Luke Sullivan,
Hey Whipple, Squeeze This:
A Guide to Creating Great Ads

CHAPTER 1
Loud & Proud

Bold or Risky Designs That Work

Creative firm
Dale Harris
Bendigo, Australia

Client
Dale Harris

Industry
Creative

Creative firm
lab303 inc.
Toronto, Canada

Client
Orange Group—Real Estate Tenant Advisory

Industry
Real Estate

Creative firm
Marko Blagojevic
Kragujevac, Serbia

Client
CrankyFish

Industry
Marketing, Web Design

Creative firm
19Blossom
Singapore

Client
Baytree Club Holdings

Industry
Food and Beverage

MC "I love the whimsy and simplicity of this mark. It has the impact of an international symbol, but the childlike proportions and hot pink color give it a fun twist that makes me want to know about the company."

RH "Does what it says, and with simplicity and wit. Not clever-clever, but with an image like this it doesn't need to be."

RM "Simple and clever. A very fun image that tells some story of a windup rhino and is told on a vibrant background.

"These guys have fun with the simplest of items. A playful and creative group."

AW "A windup rhino in pink and white—it doesn't get much more cartoonish than this!

"The out-of-proportion rendering reminds me of the wonderful manga-related plastic toys Japan has been producing in recent years."

MC "This is a very eye-catching simplification. It makes the company look smart and modern. They look as if they could probably help me with my tenant issues."

RM "The color breaks make this logo smart. The bright orange makes me think they mean business.

"It's a great concept that viewers don't need to spend any time on to understand. It just works."

AW "A delightful simplification of two words that uses color contrast as the lone contrast. If you try this approach, do check that you haven't inadvertently spelled another word in the overlap."

MC "I agree with Alex's comments below about the slightly off-putting image this mark projects. However, it did catch my eye, which isn't a bad thing in an industry as competitive as Web design.

"I do wish the black shards were bolder; they seem lost and tiny compared to the boldness of the glove/fish. Are they really even necessary?"

RM "Is it a fish? A boxing glove? Either way, it's bold and the blood-shot eyes are cranky. The black shards of glass behind the fish/glove look like the hairy arm of a boxer throwing a punch. Not sure if it's appealing to their clients, but it is memorable."

AW "Fresh idea to use a boxing glove as a fish. But a heavy attitude that does not look altogether easy to get along with describes this young design firm. Between the boxing glove, large hooded eye, and shards of black-glass-as-exhaust, it presents what I think might be a challenge to their prospective clients."

MC "The contrast between the cartoon speech bubble and the classic text type gives this mark a fun but literary feeling. It's perfect for a café that's about both chatting and reading."

RH "A nice use of empty black space and asymmetry, though the use of Clarendon throughout would have made it more cohesive. The bullet points in the line of text are somewhat large."

RM "This word balloon could easily hold together a small nuclear explosion; it's so strong and iconic. The mass of black ink around the small and delicate type almost collapses the text.

"Proportional adjustments would help this mark do an even better job and make it easier to read when used as a café store sign and in smaller applications."

AW "Asymmetry makes this mark. I wish I could see the relationship of 'wa' to the line of type beneath. There is no discernable size relationship.

"For some reason, they use two different, though very similar, sizes of type. The tail of the 'a' is fatter than the serifs on the 'w' and that's a complexity that can be removed easily."

Creative firm
Reactivity Studio
Austin, TX

Client
Oxychem Materials

Industry
Chemical Disposal and Materials Handling

Creative firm
Fauxkoi Design Company
Minneapolis, MN

Client
Fauxkoi Design Company

Industry
Design

Creative firm
Signalsmith
Johannesburg, South Africa

Client
Tsotsiboi

Industry
Clothing

Creative firm
Major Minor
Sacramento, CA

Client
Self Promotion

Industry
Design

oxychem

MC "The strength and simplicity of this mark make a strong statement about the company. The simplicity of the type works well, too. The lowercase type gives the logo a bit of warmth and friendliness that balances the serious mark."

RH "The test tube as a symbol for chemistry, though obvious, gives us a counter here in the 'O' that elegantly echoes the negative/positive space of Univers, the font below the symbol."

RM "Oxychem hopefully uses some pretty strong containers to transport those noxious materials. This logo suggests they are organized, serious, intelligent, and responsible. Seeing this on the side of a truck or on a proposal would project all the right things about a company doing serious work with a high degree of conscience."

AW "The 'O's counterspace is nicely adjusted. This mark gives credibility and reliability to this service provider."

MC "This is a very nicely balanced mark. The big, fat, tech-style monogram works well with the classical fish and scrollwork. The contrast gives me the feeling that the company may have some breadth in their design work."

AW "Very handsome use of shades of gray. Why a serif face for 'DESIGN'? Wouldn't it be more unified if it were the same face and size as 'MPLS' and 'MINN' and would then base-align with the bottoms of the lowest ribbon?"

RM "A very recognizable logo produced very well. The roughness of the face and creepiness of the eyes add more interest.

"All the type feels a bit pasted on. It's a shame the typography doesn't maintain the overall effectiveness of this logo."

AW "The rough, photocopy quality of this mark unifies art and type. Probably done digitally, it looks as if it could have been crafted off-computer, then brought in.

"'Couture' is the third part of this mark that isn't as unified, and it is sufficiently decorative to visually compete with the primary word. But at least it's got bumpy edges and the x-height is about the same height as the cap height of 'TSOTSIBOI.'

"Incidentally, *Tsotsi,* the movie, has a delightful logo, too (though not the one on the face of the DVD, which is mere typesetting)."

RM "The change from cap to lowercase for the 'j' and 'i' are a nice way to add character and soften an all-cap logo."

AW "Great idea to intrepret music visually. As background, music in a major scale tends to be bright and joyful; music in a minor scale tends to be sad or pensive. This essence has been overlooked in favor of an exploration of 'intervals.'

"If 'spaces between' are to dominate, then chopping off parts of letters would make sense. Contrasts of caps and lowercase letters are well executed; all are crafted with a common weight. 'MAJOR' appears to have more open letterspacing than 'MINOR,' which looks accidental."

Creative firm
Ellen Bruss Design
Denver, CO

Client
The Laboratory of Art and Ideas at Belmar

Industry
Art Museum

THELAB ART+IDEAS

 "I love the humor of this series. The dogs in the other three symbols are much more appealing in their typically dog-like endeavors than in the basic mark. I wish the basic dog had a bit more life. The brown and gray color palette and clean type are in tasteful contrast to the dog's indiscreet activities. THE LAB seems smart and direct."

 "The epitome of a logo being led by a strong idea. The design is cool and functional; you don't need to overdress a good concept. Is 'THELAB' supposed to be one word?

"This series illustrates how a good, strong concept can be very versatile. I can see this series being extended indefinitely without losing any of its power and humor."

 "The idea of an innocent dog sticking his nose in everyone's business is both disarming and funny. It's strongest as a series where the variations on the idea become stronger and more obvious with each new element. I would like to have seen the type treatments not trace around the circle so the type is more readable and supportive of the word-and-picture play."

 "I love this series because it is the epitome of 'risky.' Misusing a chocolate lab retriever in these four installations is a delightful twist. But it only works if you are working on behalf of an idea and art laboratory."

Creative firm
Robison Creative Studios
Springfield, MO

Client
Talent Mouse

Industry
Entertainment

MC "A mouse in shades is a great idea, but I wish this guy was simpler and had a bit more color differentiation. The sunglasses are so close to the dark red color that they're lost when the mark is small, and the thin white lines don't show at all. The type feels too small and light for the heaviness of the mark."

RM "Talent Mouse has personality and quite a confidence about him. His type may be better served below and in a face that is better balanced and reproduces well. If 'Talent Mouse' was at an angle and less flat, he may come alive and be less airplane-like."

AW "Wonderfully stylized mouse with the feel of a B-2 Spirit stealth bomber. Best part: the whiskers. This is a dynamic, fun mark."

Creative firm
Sibley Peteet Design Dallas
Dallas, TX

Client
American Heart Association

Industry
Health

MC "I like the juxtaposition of the road sign image with the lounge chair; it's a quick read that communicates the idea easily. It's nice to see a serious idea communicated with a touch of humor. It makes it less preachy. I'm going jogging now."

RH "A nice idea, executed in a lackluster manner. The chair is obviously made of four rounded rectangles and needs the same character and personality as real road signs or warning images."

AW "Though an extension of a heavily clichéd idea, this mark is initially amusing because of the unexpected placement of a stationary 'vehicle' on a road sign. It is also very well crafted."

Creative firm
Turner Duckworth
San Francisco, CA

Client
Palm

Industry
Electronics

 "The bright orange 3-D 'jellybean' circle makes this otherwise fairly typical design feel very happy and playful. It also communicates simple interactivity, which is key to the brand."

 "That this is a button indicates interaction—an appropriate idea for Palm's products. I might have tried a study in which the tops of the 'm's' were extended upward just a little so they are optically aligned with the median, waistline, or top of the x-height of the 'p' and 'a.' Curved letterforms always have to extend beyond a straight line to look equivalent."

Creative firm
Britt Funderburk
Upper Montclair, NJ

Client
TYPO.

Industry
Publishing

 "I like the design of this symbol quite a bit, but I'm not sure why there's a family or couple involved in a logo about experimental typography. It confused me a bit. It would be a great mark for something else."

 "A nicely executed visual motif."

 "I love the idea of making the negative space in the counters become visible as foreground elements. The price that must be paid to achieve this effect is by adjusting the four letterforms in height and shape. Adding to the difficulty is making the dots align vertically over the 'T' and 'Y.'"

reality digital

Creative firm
Helena Seo Design
Sunnyvale, CA

Client
RealityDigital, Inc.

Industry
Entertainment

Creative firm
Jeff Andrews Design
Salem, OR

Client
Jeff Andrews

Industry
Retail, Apparel

Creative firm
The Studio of Pius Eugene
Ho Chi Minh City, Vietnam

Client
Self Promotion

Industry
Design

Creative firm
Jeff Andrews Design
Salem, OR

Client
Conrad Coffee Company

Industry
Food and Beverage

"The monitor serving double duty as a speech bubble distinguishes this mark. Symbolism adds depth of meaning to a mark; compare this to some marks that are mere illustrations of a simple idea."

"I like the illustration of the shark boy. It's well drawn in a funny, retro way. I'm not so happy with the type. It feels like an Adobe Illustrator filter tweak rather than one done by hand with the same attention given to the shark. It should be much more nuanced and interesting, and maybe violate the edges of the circle like the shark does."

"Shark Boy is on his way. The type is inventive and well crafted and might be more expressive breaking out of the circle some.

"The colors work but seem to want to be higher-key. Less detail in the illustration will make this a better garment application image. A small label application of this would look like a bear. Keep it simple and save the complex version for the movie poster later."

"Punctuation is uncommon in logo design. The type is distorted to appear as if underwater. Very nice illustration. Two white outline thicknesses seem unnecessary; making them look the same will unify the mark. Because of embroidery's limitations, heavying the thinner line around 'Shark Boy' would probably be worthwhile. Then thin the bold, white line betwen the blue circle and the gold ring to match."

"This type stack is nicely executed—maybe too nicely. Everything is boxed in and lined up. It's supposed to be a mark for 'creative thinking,' but I'm not really seeing much creativity here—rather more order than chaos. Give me a bit more mess and unpredictability, and I'd feel it was conveying the actual process of creativity."

"A typographic solution made possible by the happy fact that most of the words in this logo are the same length. I would have been tempted to add another typographic trick to communicate the opening up of one's mind—increasing the leading as we read down the page, for example."

"This stacked treatment works. The type becomes an identifiable icon much like a theatre poster might. The content of the text suggests breaking out or discovery of possibilities, while the logo stays in the rigid box to the end. It seems there may have been a homage to change or evolution as the statement evolves, while still keeping with the simple, bold, negative spaces design."

"A very different approach in which letterforms almost become art. Note that 'CLOSE' is the only word to be chopped in half horizontally, which fills it with meaning. Unfortunately, the impact is weakened by 'MIND,' which is missing a bit along the bottom, and the much smaller ampersand. Make these competing elements 'go away' by making them agree with their surroundings so the one true focal point becomes visible."

"I love this character mark—it's fun and well drawn. Not sure I want to drink their coffee though—I might end up feeling like he looks!"

"This works, because bikers and coffee are such an unusual combination. A memorable, well-executed mark that steers clear of coffee-cup and coffee-bean clichés."

Creative firm
Sayles Graphic Design
Des Moines, IA

Client
Sports Page

Industry
Community event

MC "This would look great on the back of a leather jacket! I love the complexity and balance of bold lettering and delicate details. It has so many great references, from tattoos and playing cards to bike gangs and military insignia, all combined with talent and dexterity."

RH "A complex execution, but it's been pulled off! Gothic German Blackletter, Victorian Circus font, and tattoo motifs all combine to give a summation of biker clichés, rendered with cohesion."

RM "Kudos for putting this much detailed work into a pro bono project. There's a high degree of craftsmanship and refinement here that helps say 'This event is something special.'

"Getting all elements to read well and hold together is no small task, and this logo does a great job. It works well in black and white, driven by the likely low production budget for the event, but it would also sing in color."

AW "Wow! This mark combines seven pieces of type and one motorcycle into a single entity—and it works! Lots of value added here. Just don't make it too small, or the sponsors won't be legible."

 "The drawing style of the bull and rider are wonderful and eccentric. The big red dot helps to make the thin lines stand out visually. The mark has an artistic quality that makes me think the developers care about the history of the area, not just about building houses.

"I wish the line weights in the type had as much variation and life as the mark. Hand lettering rather than a typeface would have been a better choice here."

 "Great visual storytelling here. The illustration quality is unique, though very delicate for the massive circle that contains it. It will be difficult to use in some applications, and that could have been avoided with different line weights.

"While it's memorable and visually rich, it seems out of place for a real estate company and their need to demonstrate stability, confidence, and such. A different, cleaner typeface for the name could have helped establish more business confidence."

 "A well-reasoned solution that has led to an interesting logo. I would have preferred to see a more freehand approach taken to the lettering, and I'm not sure the underline is really necessary. Simplify where possible."

 "This is an ideal solution to the circumstances described in the designer's statement. There is meaning to each of the qualities—the wiggliness throughout and the brick red color—and decisions in this creative result. This is a solution to a well-defined problem, and thoroughly defining a problem always makes knowing when you are done much more evident."

Creative firm
Fresh Oil
Pawtucket, RI

Client
Blackstone Studios

Industry
Real Estate

 The Reverend Blackstone was a quirky outcast in his day. He traveled on a white bull, often reading and writing as he went.

This symbol for Blackstone Studios, a work-live space for artists, looks as if it may have been rendered on one of those bumpy rides. The terra-cotta color hints of the numerous red-brick mills that, along with the studios, line the Blackstone River.

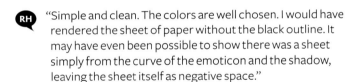

Creative firm
Roskelly, Inc.
Portsmouth, RI

Client
WinkFlash

Industry
Photo Prints

RH "Simple and clean. The colors are well chosen. I would have rendered the sheet of paper without the black outline. It may have even been possible to show there was a sheet simply from the curve of the emoticon and the shadow, leaving the sheet itself as negative space."

AW "Perfect! The intentionally tight letterspacing makes the name a wordmark rather than mere typesetting, and the color change makes a word space redundant."

Creative firm
Britt Funderburk
Upper Montclair, NJ

Client
Nicholson

Industry
Full Service Digital Agency

MC "I'm guessing that a 'full service digital agency' is something like a service bureau? If so, I love the squares even more for their tie-in to pixels. The simplicity of this mark gives a very professional, corporate feeling to the company. They may not have a sense of humor, but their work will be perfect every time."

RH "The central position of the vertical strokes within each diamond, terminating at the diamond's midline, is very elegant. Positive and negative space in complete harmony."

RM "So much is gotten out of so little in this mark, in the way the 'N' is created so that the two squares take on new duties. It's always a pleasure to see, both as a designer and as a viewer. This is a logo that will age well over time. Even its colors work without being trend-driven."

AW "A really good logo must, in my opinion, use—or at least acknowledge—negative space. The 'N' doesn't actually exist at all in this mark. It is the familiar shape we recognize when the black and blue squares, with their missing chunks, are positioned just so."

Creative firm
Britt Funderburk
Upper Montclair, NJ

Client
Hammerschön GmbH

Industry
Manufacturing

 "Hits the nail on the head. This is a great example of 'less is more.' There is nothing extra here, and everything that is here works—even the color."

 "A simple, straightforward idea, but an entirely appropriate one for a no-nonsense hammer supplier. The red color is again suitably straightforward. The curves on the claw end of the hammer could be more flowing."

 "An example of a genre of marks in which a simplified image is inserted into the negative space of a letterform. It forces imagery to become space. The trick is to simplify the image so it acts as negative space without oversimplifying it, causing it to lose its distinctive character for that specific client."

Creative firm
Robison Creative Studios
Springfield, MO

Client
Kidz Kamp

Industry
Camp and Recreation

 "I like the enthusiasm of the boy's head. It communicates fun and eagerness quite well. The body adds nothing to the communication. The head alone would work better as a symbol. It needs something more to communicate the idea of camp."

 "We have a stylistic mismatch between the way the head and the hands are executed."

 "This is a charming illustration, but it makes me wonder where the line between an illustration and a mark is.

"I think a representational mark, one that may be first perceived as an illustration, has to be viewed repeatedly to register as an identifying symbol. If this rendering had two 'K's for fingers, representing 'Kidz Kamp,' it would become more of a symbol. Also, color use must mean something: if two out of three clothes are in color, why is the hat evidently made of flesh?"

Creative firm
The Decoder Ring
Austin, TX

Client
Austin Museum of Art

Industry
Museum

 "This is a rip on lots of street art, but that's what makes the connection to New York work. It's a rat, not the Statue of Liberty for a change! I hope this was for a show about New York street art, or I rescind my compliments."

 "Looks like it was authentically spray painted using a mask. That's the essential quality it must achieve."

Creative firm
Dale Harris
Bendigo, Australia

Client
Blank Expression

Industry
Music, Entertainment

 "This feels more like artwork for a T-shirt or a skateboard than a logo meant to last. But I'd wear the T-shirt."

 "A fusion of found parts—an 'x,' wings, and hairy tails— all damaged by age. The designer has imbued this mark with attitude, which is necessary in the music and entertainment industry."

Creative firm
Stacy Karzen
Chicago, IL

Client
Andy Nebel

Industry
Public Relations

 "This is a nice poke at PR puffery. The pump and the main type are nicely drawn and relate well to each other. The smaller type feels like an afterthought both in style and placement."

 "Verticality and the gray color unify the illustration and the type in this humorous mark for a public relations consultant. There is a slight lack of agreement between 'COMPANY' and 'Nebel.' This is a consequence of properly matching the size of 'COMPANY' with 'THE.' But this cascading logic is all predicated on tucking 'THE' just so in between the ascenders of 'Andy.' Is that sufficient benefit to cause another problem?

"One solution is to size 'COMPANY' to fit beneath 'Nebel' and work with 'THE' to match, including adjusting length of ascenders in 'Andy Nebel.'"

Creative firm
Niedermeier Design
Seattle, WA

Client
Intava Corporation

Industry
Retail Enhancement Technology

 "Friendly and professional. This is a very nice symbol that conveys a strong feeling of modern professionalism without being sterile or cold. I like the type too, but I wish there was a stronger relationship of weight and shape between the type and the symbol."

 "A nice illustration of a touch screen in action, using the first two letters of the company name. It's simple and it communicates.

"The gray and green are appropriate—fresh but reliable, not too hip or whimsical. The custom type is set a wee bit too tight, and the 'ta' and 'va' pairs more loosely than the others."

 "A letter 'i' can be abstracted into a figure and a computer console. The remarkable thing is that, by carefully adjusting the negative space, the letter 'N' is present, but not at all recognizable."

Creative firm
PS Cali, Inc.
Los Angeles, CA

Client
Renata Helfman

Industry
Retail

Creative firm
Turner Duckworth Design
London, UK

Client
The Fresh Olive Company

Industry
Food

Creative firm
Highway77 Design
Northford, CT

Client
Self Promotion

Industry
Design

Creative firm
Espial
Johannesburg, South Africa

Client
Vukani

Industry
Gaming

MC "I love the hand-drawn flow of this script. It feels like it grew that way naturally. The space between the 'V' and 'e' is a bit too tight, but otherwise everything about this logo makes me happy."

RH "Bit more air between the 'V' and the 'e,' please. Otherwise, lovely—warm, well executed, friendly, organic. And without any hessian textures or tea stenciling."

RM "This is a great take on the idea of being green (*vert* is French for 'green'). It's very beautiful and modern, yet hand-painted. I get the feeling that the store shows that items can be eco-friendly without being 'earthy' or 'crunchy.'"

AW "Feminine, organic, lovely letterforms."

MC "I love the hand-as-tree to communicate 'handmade.' I wish it were bigger though. The type overpowers the art.

"There is a struggle going on between the rough shapes, like the olive and the ground, and the super-smooth shapes, like the hills and the type. For the rough direction to really work, it should be rougher and more handmade. It feels a bit undecided."

RH "A nice, simple idea, executed in the German poster style of Lucian Bernhard. There is a slight discrepancy between the smoothness of the type and the shape of the olive, and the colors could be punchier. The hand/tree could also benefit from being larger in the overall composition, maybe in a squarer layout."

AW "An arm as a tree trunk is a compelling juxtaposition. There is a roughness to the olive and the black silhouette, which makes them seem just a bit out of place, given the extreme sleekness of the other elements."

MC "This mark mixes metaphors in a very elegant way. Rough meets smooth, fancy meets plain, road sign meets wine label. It will never work when small due to the small script type, but I love the use of empty space."

AW "How to translate a clichéd symbol—a highway sign—into your own mark? Process it heavily and don't put big numerals on it! A spelled-out script number is fresh."

MC "This mark is a wonderfully executed riff on classic playing card art. It communicates the South African connection superbly with the mask, dot pattern, and leaves, while the spade and banner communicate gaming, powerfully, in any culture."

RH "Nice execution of a neat idea. Everyone is familiar with the ornate ace of spades, and this incorporates other elements without losing that central conceit. However, I'm not sure what those other elements mean—leaves and a tiki mask? Still, it's memorable and technically well done."

AW "A good mark should communicate on a subconscious level. This one does. Cover the type and you can feel what it represents. Interesting combination of stylized and natural leaf shapes."

Creative firm
Refinery Design Company
Dubuque, IA

Client
Home Health Care

Industry
Health Care

Creative firm
Refinery Design Company
Dubuque, IA

Client
Dupaco Community Credit Union

Industry
Financial

> Dupaco Community Credit Union created The Green Saver Challenge to educate children about the importance of recycling.

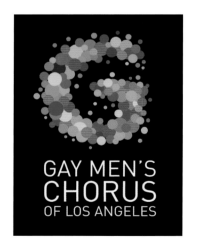

Creative firm
Ian Lynam Design
Tokyo, Japan

Client
Signatures Network for Taproot

Industry
Music

Creative firm
Top Design
Los Angeles, CA

Client
Gay Men's Chorus of Los Angeles

Industry
Nonprofit

"While I've seen this type of design before, this one works pretty well. I wish the cross was not attached to the side of the house. It makes the design seem unbalanced and tilted."

 "A nice example of a simple figure/ground, positive/negative relationship in a logo. The concept—a health care cross in a house—is very straightforward, but the elegant execution carries the simple idea."

 "Tasty use of figure and ground, without the need for line. The process of making a mark for health care provided in the home is achieved, quite naturally, by adding a symbol for house plus a symbol for health care. I wonder whether a similar result can be achieved, for example, for a handyman or a home inspection service?"

 "Nice, strong linework. A sense of power and energy in the figure, and a simple, compact arrangement that would work well on T-shirts, badges, and the like. It should appeal to children without resorting to kiddie clichès.

"The color is somewhat weak—the white drop shadow is more 'forward in the mix' than the type, a design no-no; and the green is too tonally similar to the background orange, making it 'fizz' uncomfortably."

 "Terrific and easily adjusted for one-color use: 'GREEN' and 'SAVER' in black, and drop out all other colors."

 "Great name for a band and this font and tree/root system work well together. This is a memorable mark, but the success is that the simple yet rough artwork will reproduce well on band T-shirts and photocopied venue flyers."

 "The idea of inverting a tree into a root is fun. But how much artistic freedom is the right amount? Strictly speaking, a *taproot* is a straight-tapering root growing vertically downward and forming the center from which subsidiary rootlets spring. (A perfect example of this is a carrot freshly pulled from the soil with its rootlets still intact.) So, while there is nothing wrong with this solution, there may be a little more that could be right about it; there must be a tree that grows more like an inverted carrot than this one.

"Also, if every rock band uses Blackletter, is it a sign of hard-edged rebelliousness or simple me-tooism? And does it say anything about the differences in their music?"

 "This looks more like a logo for a kid's party than a chorus. Why dots? Why a 'G'?"

 "Typographically clean and simple. Visually fun and expressive on many levels. My only question is why a 'G'? This collection of dots/voices could easily define more creative shapes or letters."

 "Reminiscent of the tests for color blindness developed by Dr. Shinobu Ishihara in 1917, this mark presumably uses all the colors in the rainbow for more self-descriptive purposes."

Creative firm
The Decoder Ring
Austin, TX

Client
Carolina Panthers Chefs
Association

Industry
NFL

Logo for use on in-house apparel and collateral materials for the NFL's Carolina Panthers Chefs Association. The group informally refers to themselves as "The Dirty Kitchen Rats," and requested a mark that represented them more accurately than the crest bestowed upon them by the league.

MC "This is nicely executed, funny, and smart. The play with negative space works very well, and the weights all work. It's a very subtle touch to have the eyes made from asymmetrical icons when everything else is perfectly symmetrical. If I were a DKR, I'd want it on my toque."

RH "Rats in the kitchen—an edgy idea treated in an edgy way. The negative- space skull is beautifully executed. Technically balanced and beautifully done. A winner."

RM "A gross name that evokes disgusting images. But this logo brings it all to light and makes you laugh. Then it goes further and adds the skull, complete with a cleaver and bottle from the kitchen. It's eye-catching, witty, and produced very well. What more could you want?"

AW "This mark is tattoo worthy. Love the skull resulting from the negative space between the rats, and the kitchen utensils as the skull's eyes."

Creative firm
Campbell-Ewald
Warren, MI

Client
Self Promotion

Industry
Advertising

Creative firm
Jeff Fisher LogoMotives
Portland, OR

Client
Triangle Productions!

Industry
Theater, Performing Arts

RH "Definitely a 'Detroit-looking' logo. Typographically, the 'CAMPBELL-EWALD' could be better if the arc was centered over the center of the logo as a whole, rather than shifted down and to the right."

AW "Blackletter with gear teeth, representing the automotive manufacturing capital of the world, distinguishes this mark. Though not precisely cutting edge, it is worthwhile for its use of what looks like real metal. The use of authentic elements, rather than computer-generated simulations, adds tremendously to achieving a distinctive mark."

RH "This logo gets its power from the title and those three stars. As an execution, I can't help but feel it would have been more effective to cut the shapes out of paper for real. That would have given it even more immediacy."

AW "Yes, the implication in this mark is provocative. But formally, the three asterisks are the most potent characteristic. In fact, if the word were spelled out, it would be a less interesting mark than it is now. Symbols can replace letters in less rude words for the same effect.

"I wish I knew why the front wheel has those little black shards—it is so atypical in this design that it should have meaning. Maybe if I'd seen the play, I'd get it."

Creative firm
Glitschka Studios
Salem, OR

Client
Jim Henson Company

Industry
TV Production

Creative firm
Glitschka Studios
Salem, OR

Client
Little Chimp Society

Industry
Illustration Marketplace

Creative firm
Atomic Design
Crowley, TX

Client
Liquidator/Paula Monthie

Industry
Estate Sales

Creative firm
Korn Design
Boston, MA

Client
Sage Hospitality Group

Industry
Hotel

MC This logo takes the 60s Filmore style and has a fabulously whacky time with it! The lettering is nicely drawn and spaced, and the goofy containing shape is just wonderful. I particularly like the feet."

RH "Playful and fun, but still beautifully executed. The 'Austin Powers' logo was a very visible example of a psychedelic logo poorly executed, but this—the colors, the type—pulls it all together effortlessly. The 'The' slowly sinking into the top is a lovely touch."

RM "Hilarious! This is more than just a logo for a puppet show; it's also a strange little puppet itself. It's very well executed and will reproduce clearly on kids' T-shirts, toys, games, and, of course, puppets."

AW "'The' is in the process of being absorbed by the 'Skrumps'— a delightful, kid-sensitive treatment. That Henson's Muppets caught the imagination of the American television public in the late 1960s is referenced in the funky psychedelic lettering and color combination."

MC "This is a nicely drawn monkey—cheerful and welcoming. I love his face, too; maybe Paul Frank could use some help."

RH "Good, strong, iconc illustration; nice color choice. Will work well at small sizes on the Web. I'd have engineered a way to keep the linewidths on the paws more equal (or even completely equal, natch)."

RM "Very fun and illustrative icon for an illustrative group. I'm sure all their members appreciate an icon as fun as the group's name. I enjoy seeing this 'little chimp' much more than just seeing the acronym 'LCS' on their website."

LIQUIDATOR

MC "This is the Godzilla of type treatments—big, fat, and bold. I almost missed the drip the first time I saw it though. I think it should be bigger and 'juicier' to stand out and contrast with the super-extreme, heavy-duty type."

AW "What makes this work is combining letterforms and an illustrative element in which the letters dominate, but the minor illustration adds the meaning. This has a slight 'yuck factor,' and it really is an illuminaton of the word's meaning rather than an expression of the business's actual purpose."

MC "This logo is sweetly simple and nostalgic without being complicated. It's a perfect blend of type styles. It makes me miss linoleum and lemon meringue pie!"

RH "For me, putting 'the' on the same baseline would have been better—either that, or centering the type on a horizontal line—than reducing the ascender of the 'h' to match the cap height of 'Curtis.' At the moment, the 'the' doesn't know which way to go."

AW "Wonderful simplicity and expressive typographic contrast. It hints at vintage 50s/60s design, and the colors are impressive: orange and brown are closely related.

"A design can be considered 'done' when nothing can be changed—even a little bit—without damaging the overall result. This is such a design."

Creative firm
MINE
San Francisco, CA

Client
Brainfloss

Industry
Career Services

Creative firm
Dale Harris
Bendigo, Australia

Client
Madman Entertainment/Bollywood Masala

Industry
Entertainment

Creative firm
Hoffi
Cardiff, UK

Client
Self Promotion

Industry
Design

Creative firm
Smoky Mirrors.com
Bronx, NY

Client
Self Promotion

Industry
Print, Design, Comic Books, Entertainment

 **Brain**floss

(MC) "This is so close it hurts. The squiggle isn't quite a brain, so it can't be used on its own without the type. That's too bad! Adding the drop shadow is a nice touch that makes a 2-D object seem to be 3-D. The type is nice too, although possibly a bit small depending on the application."

(RH) "I didn't immediately see that as a floating brain, just a scribble. It would be better if the scribble reflected the whorls of the brain more—without losing its casual immediacy."

(RM) "This is a cute, simple idea. It's not overdone, but maybe a few more details in the brain would've made it more complete. Overall, a nice concept as long as the type stays near the mark to define what's going on."

(AW) "The floating brain, indicated by the oval shadow, is a nice approach. The semi-serif type is modern and tasteful.

"That there are two other squiggly shapes made in Illustrator in this chapter speaks to the need for a more distinctive treatment. 'Brain' plus 'floss' can equal something better than a ball of pseudo-yarn. What is the most extreme way of showing an idea? What will make it memorable and your client's own mark that cannot be copied?"

(MC) "What a great opportunity for lettering with some spirit and exoticism! The mark here feels very 'computer layered' and not well related to the type. The type feels stiff and static when it could move and play with much more grace and character.

"There are so many wonderful references that could have been used for this. This feels too obvious and limited."

(RM) "Striking and entertaining colors and imagery. Type seems 'off.' It's not quite playful and fun, but not quite formal and straight. I wish it were more one than the other and not just uncomfortable."

(AW) "The Indian connection is conveyed in the sacred water lily (*Nelumbo nucifera*), but the real character in this mark is delivered by the informal type treatment with the uneven baseline and inverted and mirrored lowercase 'g' standing in as a 'b' and 'd.'"

(MC) "This mark has a beautiful, understated elegance to it, especially through its off-center placement in the circle. The thin swashes on the 'H' are a bit rough. If those details were smoothed out, this logo would really sing!"

(RH) "Technically beautiful. The loop outside the circle is elegantly done. There seems to be some wonkiness in the curves; could this be from the original font? The 'H' is too close to the 'o.'"

(AW) "Perfect circle + elegant type + hairline contrast with solid circle + off-centeredness = tasty mark."

Jammer

(RH) "For once, the relevant choice of Blackletter, with its repeating geometry, makes this work where other fonts would have failed."

(RM) "A good example of an ambigram. Some of the tight letterspacing causes some tension points, but overall, it's a challenging project that's been well executed. The small curls on the 'e' add a touch of character."

(AW) "Both the positive and the negative shapes have been carefully manipulated, as Langdon would teach. So this mark is a worthy interpretation of his work.

"The gothic treatment, based on German Blackletter forms, might have been chosen for its extra meaning. But perhaps, Blackletter characters lend themselves to manipulation into new shapes because they are less familiar and can be bent and twisted more freely than, say, Helvetica."

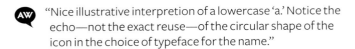

Creative firm
Alambre Estudio
Donostia, Spain

Client
Self Promotion

Industry
Design

 "Reminiscent of spooled paper on a press, or of a rotated barcode or CD, thus evoking both the traditional form of print and the digital form."

 "Nice illustrative interpretation of a lowercase 'a.' Notice the echo—not the exact reuse—of the circular shape of the icon in the choice of typeface for the name."

Creative firm
Calagraphic Design
Elkins Park, PA

Client
The Hurricane Poster Project

Industry
Fundraising, Katrina victims and Red Cross support, Retail

RH "Milton Glaser's iconic 'I [heart] NY' logo is given an appropriately gritty appropriation here, with the state of Louisiana doubling as the 'L.' Very nice use of a limited red and black palette."

AW "Post Hurricane Katrina, any logo representing NoLa had better be dirty. I see why this mark, designed for a poster, was adapted for purchasable items. I'd wear it."

Creative firm
Turner Duckworth
San Francisco, CA

Client
Popchips

Industry
Food

 "This is a nice use of negative space that adds some fun to lettering. The missing 'o' and 'i' mess with your eyes and give the mark character."

 "A nice use of positive/negative space that has a relevance to the product. More animated bounce might help (although that is somewhat of a cliché in snack lettering). It looks somewhat formal as is. The white line clipping the 'c' indicates there may be even more invisible white elements to be found if we looked more closely."

 "Proportional thickness defines the ring of the 'o' and the circle around the smaller dot—a sign of the designer's control over every detail of this tasty mark."

Creative firm
Lloyds Graphics Design, Ltd
Blenheim, New Zealand

Client
Rapaura Springs 2

Industry
Wine

 "A nice blend of modernity, organic natural shapes, and elegance."

 "This wine better be as good as the logo. It sets a smart and sophisticated foundation and would be a dramatic execution on labels with endless possibilities for print techniques, none of which would destroy the rock solid foundation for the simple graphic. This logo will work as well in ten years as it does today."

 "A flower made out of stones? Strings or a stream? Beautiful shapes take priority over simple letterforms, though the type is on top. If the red color is chosen for the winery's excellent red wines, gray must represent their fine pinot gris?"

Creative firm
Fauxkoi Design Company
Minneapolis, MN

Client
Catlick Records

Industry
Music

Creative firm
Myles Delfin
Makati City, Philippines

Client
Empanada Republic

Industry
Novelty Bakery

Creative firm
Artiva Design
Genova, Italy

Client
Ton Mobel

Industry
Audio Design

Creative firm
David Maloney
St. Louis Park, MN

Client
Semi Studio Systems

Industry
TV Studio Design

"I like the slightly psycho feeling of this cat icon. It definitely has a retro 'Felix the Cat' feeling to it, which makes me think the company might have some revival rock on their label. I like the lightning-bolt-shaped edges of the cat's face but wish the dot of the 'i' was heavier, less of a cliché shape and tied in with the icon better."

 "The retro-cool feeling of this logo takes you to a place you've been before in your mind—a place of old cartoons and black and white comics.

"When you look more closely at the final execution you want to rework the contours and have the licking tongue become a more memorable feature. The logo was likely created at too large a size, with too much detail."

 "The two typefaces contrast quite purposefully here. The only thing they have in common is their width. They contrast in posture, case, size, and style.

"Nice relationship of line weight between 'RECORDS' and the cat's whiskers. I suspect the top script is a typeface rather than having been hand drawn: the 'c' overlap isn't quite smooth."

 "Technically, the dashed lines should terminate with one whole dash, not the little bitty ones we have here. Should the character not be looking at the empanada and looking happier?"

 "The client's goal of upscaling street food was realized by both the bright, simple coloring and the unicameral typeface (a typeface which mixes caps and lowercase into a single character set) used in 'empanada.'

"Only the 'P' and 'D' are capitals—interesting that they alone would have ascenders or descenders if set in lowercase letters—so only those two letters had to have their weight adjusted when reduced in size to match the x-height of the neighboring lowercase letters."

 "Flipping the diaeresis on the 'O' is a nice touch."

 "Nice use of negative shapes. Typographically sound. A very solid logo at any size."

"This is an excellent example of the saying: 'It isn't what typeface you choose; it's how you use the typeface you've chosen.' Extra tight letter and line spacing are the activated relationships that make this mark visible."

 "A happy coincidence of modular product and three repeating initials. The colors are unusual but very effective."

 "Another mark-as-diagram example. That the actual shapes of the product are quarter circles and the name of the company has three 'S's is wonderful. One test of genius is when the result appears inevitable. This mark is an inevitable result of the specific attributes of the client. Tasty color choices, too."

Creative firm
Fauxkoi Design Company
Minneapolis, MN

Client
Catlick Records

Industry
Music

 "This logo could easily have fallen prey to over-detailing and confusing embellishment. Instead, a great balance of well-unified elements makes this a strong mark with a lot of personality.

"The high-touch printmaking execution is bulletproof, holding up well when translated to band paraphernalia and marketing materials."

 "Interesting that this mark uses a Cyrillic 'De,' equivalent to our Latin 'D.' I get the gothic overtones, but that Cyrillic letter is intriguing. Nice that the spontaneous splattering is not symmetrical."

Creative firm
Jeff Andrews Design
Salem, OR

Client
Sugar Frosted Goodness!

Industry
Illustration Website

RH "Choosing one style for a site that represents a range of illustrators (or any visually minded group) is always difficult. Having a male as your mascot also may not fit everyone, though this may indeed be for an all-male group of vector illustrators that like pencils! Who knows?

"The brave covering of the 'G' is permissible, as the full three letters can be seen on the character's T-shirt."

AW "Love the abstraction of the 'SFG' by being hidden. But I can't see any relationship beyond proximity between the front and back halves. If the pencil's tip was as stubby as the weight of the letters behind, there could be a conceptual connection."

Creative firm
KFR Communications, LLC
New Egypt, NJ

Client
North Gate Ministry

Industry
Recreation

 "Skaters would connect with the energy of this logo and the street-made feeling. I could see the figure in a second color on top of everything else, making it less flat and more active."

 "Careful overlaps and enough splatters to make it look youthful and 'skateboardy.' Note that there's no obvious religious reference shown, so this becomes an emblem of 'belonging'—probably a powerful attractant to the target audience."

Creative firm
Robison Creative Studios
Springfield, MO

Client
Royale Builders

Industry
Construction

 "I assume this building company has a list of very high-class clients. Typographically, the centered layout does emphasize the fact that 'ROYALE' and 'BUILDERS' are not the same length, and the designer has had to alter the letterspacing to accomodate this. I wonder if there would be a better solution—stacking the two words beneath, for example—that would obviate this inelegant necessity."

 "Royal Builders looks like Royal Gourmet Chocolates— and I want some. Have them redo my entire kitchen in chocolate, please.

"The center carrier shape has a lot of depth and richness. The small detail in the cartouches will undoubtedly be a problem reproduced on the builder pickup trucks or on the side of his hard hat."

 "Love the crown most of all. Quite a distinctive mark, especially for a builder. But if you cover the word 'BUILDERS,' what does this enterprise do? If you can't tell, then the mark may not convey enough nonverbal meaning."

babyfirst

Creative firm
Mad Studios
Hong Kong, China

Client
babyfirst

Industry
Retail

Babyfirst sells high-end childcare products in Mainland China. The client wanted to convey the company's "foreign origin" but cater to local tastes and cultures. The Chinese government encourages families to have one child, hence the single swaddled "HUG ME!" baby, communicating the preciousness of an only child. It is a Chinese tradition to swaddle a newborn baby in red to confer good fortune on it. The pacifier communicates well-being.

MC "Time was clearly spent making this baby icon well drawn and sweet. The pacifier is a great touch. Too bad they didn't spend more time spacing the type."

RH "A nice execution of a simple idea. The baby owes a bit too much to the ellipse tool in Illustrator, and more organic yet still-graphic curves would have given it more life and character. Still, a nice design."

AW "The designer's statement explains a reason for everything on this logo: baby, singularity, arms outstretched for hugging, red color, and pacifier. In the face of such clear thinking, who can quibble with the 'yfi' and 'rst' ligatures?"

camp242

Creative firm
Eye Design Studio
Charlotte, NC

Client
Warehouse 242 :: a church for the city

Industry
Church

Creative firm
Sayles Graphic Design
Des Moines, IA

Client
Campbell's Nutrition

Industry
Food

RH "A nice interplay of old and new, though the 'C' in the star could have been better positioned so that the top left cropped either in or out rather than just nick the edge."

RM "The clash between the classic star and the ornate pattern creates a beautiful logo mark here. The simple lowercase type stays out of the way, yet remains highly legible and complementary. The logo communicates a feeling of old values in a new context of tradition with modernity."

AW "Two primary contrasts make this mark work: the curvilinear shapes of the 'C' within the angular star, and the two weights of type. Nice that the white space is allowed to infiltrate the star's perimeter. A border would have killed that activity and made the star more dominant than the 'C.' As it is, they are in near equilibrium."

MC "This logo feels like a modern update of a classic from the turn of the century (the last one). It retains a natural feeling in spite of the clean, flat graphic treatment which gives the company a sense of history.

"It looks like the carrot and 'C' could be pulled out as a separate icon that would work on its own, too. The script type is nicely done, and all the details balance well. Nice job."

RH "This is interesting and very nearly works. A combination of 60s geometric greenery and block typography, rendered in bold green and orange (and black). The carrot is too basic compared to the rest of the design and could have been done with more definition and detail, and 'NUTRITION,' in a flimsy letterspaced serif, seems to have snuck in from another design.

"The ruler-and-compass curves need some smoothing throughout as well, but somewhere under all that there's an eye-catching design."

"Trashbags" are purses made by hand from recycled and scrap materials. Though every bag is unique, they are all characterized by quilted patches constructed from old, plastic shopping bags. The Trashbag logo was designed to recall thread and convey a sense of carefree, quirky elegance. A gestural scribble is paired with an abstraction of a handle to create a funky purse icon, which flows into the logotype. The script typeface is a custom design.

Creative firm
The Decoder Ring
Austin, TX

Client
Boost Mobile, Inc. and Cornerstone Media

Industry
Communications

Creative firm
The Whole Package
Fort Collins, CO

Client
Leila Singleton

Industry
Fashion

Creative firm
Dotzero Design
Portland, OR

Client
Tree Leaf Music

Industry
Music

Creative firm
Calagraphic Design
Elkins Park, PA

Client
Calagraphic Design

Industry
Political

RH "I'd have liked an icon to go with this."

RM "A bold and blockhead logo. It looks like a tattoo on the arm of a band's roadie. This logo conveys tons of character yet is executed soundly."

AW "Delicious modernist characters that lack curves are set on a curve—a wonderful contrast. These letterforms harken to Germanic Blackletter without actually being Blackletter."

MC "I like where this logo almost gets. The idea of a scribble that's also a purse is great, but this lettering and the scribble look awkward, like they were drawn with a mouse and not by hand. Imperfection can be great, so why not push it and do it by hand (the way the purses are made)?"

AW "The designer's statement is complete, and the mark reaches every one of her goals. Still, the handle of the purse is unresolved, because it has nothing in common with the rest of the mark; it contrasts in color, weight, shape, and line quality.

"Balancing contrast with similarity is the true goal of relating design form, so having more in common would make that particular handle the 'right' treatment. That I can accidentally read 'frashbags' is a smaller quibble, because I like 'frashbags.'"

RH "A neat little idea—soundwaves and leaf spokes. Typographically, the 'L' is too wide, the 'RE' and 'AF' too close together, and the ruler-and-compass constructon and rounded end strokes don't seem to be of the same style as the leaf itself.

"The paler sound waves have a kink in the center due to the curves not being smoothed out sufficiently; in fact, it may even be a more elegant logo if the lighter waves were dropped completely. The concept would still be there."

RM "The way the leaf and the tree images both get equal play and complement each other well is the real success behind this logo. The colors also work to unify the mark, and the type is stable and appropriate with or without the logo accompanying it. It works well on many levels."

AW "Love, love, love the leaf. Relating the art to type through the use of color is excellent. But does the use of two fonts add anything? Why couldn't 'MUSIC' be set in the same face as 'TREE LEAF'? To the extent that it distracts from the leaf art, it is a wrong choice. One word set in a smaller size is arguably more distinctive than the one word set in brown, so there is an unnecessary competition in hierarchy."

RH "Appropriate use of 'Block' for the text; it nicely matches the photocopied and worn nature of the illustration."

RM "The non-designed quality of this logo makes it work well. It's about the idea, while the execution stays simple and almost crude. I want to see the word 'VOTE' larger and almost with an exclamation point at the end."

AW "I completely agree with the sentiment of this mark: participate! But that is either one huge donkey or one youthful elephant. The relationship made in the shared girth of their waists is right thinking, but the result appears to emphasize the donkey. That is probably unintentional. Or it is an insiduously subconscious political message?"

Creative firm
DogStar
Birmingham, AL

Client
DogStar

Industry
Design

 "I love this lucky dog mark. It's fun and funny and great as part of the Dogstar holiday series. Nicely drawn, too."

 "This logo has a beautiful balance of positive and negative—the eyes and nose have a similar weight, shape, and character as the clover's 'inlets' and stem, giving it a stylistic cohesion.

"The top two leaves nicely double as ears in a simple an non-contrived manner, with just the right degree of whimsical 'flop.' Finally, the simple green color scheme is all that is needed."

 "If you don't see the stem as a tongue, you may not see the dog at all. That suggests the combination of dog plus lucky clover is skewed slightly too much toward the clover."

Creative firm
Alambre Estudio
Donostia, Spain

Client
Luma Industrias S.A.

Industry
Motorcycle Locking Systems

 "I'd love to see how this one was applied. It's an aggressive mark that seems perfect for the motorcycle market. The pointy ears and Fu Manchu mustache give it a slightly devilish quality that works."

 "This bouncer is precisely the kind of guy I'd want to protect my hog. The mirroring of the eyebrows and mustache reveal a good relationship, creating design sensitivity."

Creative firm
Coastlines Creative Group
Vancouver, Canada

Client
Hotwears

Industry
Clothing, Accessory

 "Elegance is the absence of complexity. Note the precision with which 'WARMTH YOU CAN WEAR' aligns with 'WEARS.' And I think the flame has a slight suggestion of the letter 'H.' Overall, very nicely unified."

Creative firm
Masood Ahmed
Bronx, NY

Client
Reds BBQ

Industry
Restaurant

 "Hot food? Compact urban mark that has a touch of Deco diner to it. I can see this working well on shirts, bags, and menus.

"Typographically, the addition of dots between the 'BBQ' letters on the right would help overcome the lack of symmetry (four letters versus three), and curving the actual letters of 'BRONX' rather than just the baseline would have been more elegant."

 "A fitting solution for a Bronx eatery that makes its claim from being hot and in the Bronx. The use of the thermometer suggests temperature hot, which seems a bit off from the hot flavor of BBQ they might want to suggest."

 "This mark seems about 20 percent too busy, so what is the most likely candidate for editing? 'BRONX' gets my vote; it doesn't agree enough. Delete the word and its U-shaped stripe and embed the word over the street signs. The added benefit is the thermometer's bulb then hangs down in all its roundness and true importance."

Creative firm
David Clark Design
Tulsa, OK

Client
Cherry Street Association

Industry
Tourism

Creative firm
Niedermeier Design
Seattle, WA

Client
Intellitax

Industry
Accounting

 "This is a clean, simple icon that really doesn't need type to communicate."

 "Street and cherry—a simple combo drawn directly from the name. You can't argue with that, though I wonder why the cherry is slightly larger. It might have been nice to try a photo of a real cherry, which may have stopped this design from sliding into slight dullness."

"This mark is fine as far as it goes, which is my way of saying this looks fairly generic. A diagrammatic approach such as this needs character. If that can't be invented, maybe more than a diagram is called for. Maybe a photograph of a stem? Or a photo of a cherry on top of a photo of a traffic light— anything for an unexpected twist on what is a basically good idea— so the client can 'own' the mark."

"This is a very nicely designed mark that sets exactly the right tone. The international-symbol simplicity is perfect for a software product, and the gray matter defined by numbers gets the mathematical/accounting aspect across elegantly and succinctly. Even if the details of the smaller numbers are lost a bit at very small sizes, there is enough information left to make it work."

"Accounting software is interpreted as a brain—which is literally gray matter!—with numbers. The spacing of the numerals and their modest abstraction is handled sensitively."

Creative firm
Lloyds Graphics Design, Ltd
Blenheim, New Zealand

Client
Bike & Walk Marlborough

Industry
Nonprofit

 "The feet/bike chain part of this mark is very clever and eye-catching. I wish the application to the googie shape and type had been better thought out. The type is crying out to be stacked less rigidly, especially when joined with the asymmetrical googie shape.

"If the type was less lined up, 'bike' wouldn't have to be smaller than 'walk', and the ampersand could also be a more comfortable size."

 "A neat concept, well executed. I wonder if we had flipped it whether we could also have had a 'W' for walk instead of an 'M.'

"The type is a little airy, mainly due to the ascenders on 'walk.' Caps may have worked better, though using a rounded style in keeping with the image is an excellent point of continuity."

 "The bike-links-turned-feet concept has legs! The eye wants to linger on the links-turned-feet illustration more than the television shape they're in or the rather bloopy type that changes character as it get bigger and smaller. While those would be improvements, the sign of a good concept is that it's hard to kill, and this one survives the day. The people of Marlborough have an event they can be proud to participate in."

 "Nice combo of feet and bike chain! The type suffers from size-itis; as type is enlarged or reduced, its weight also changes, so these four sizes of type have four different weights. A logo needs to be handled differently and with greater care than the typesetting of a headline in a magazine, where speediness mitigates casual craft.

"Also, does the ampersand deserve the visibility it receives from the contrasting green color? Seems a black plus sign would blend in and put the emphasis back where it belongs: on the sweet artwork."

Creative firm
M3 Advertising Design
Las Vegas, NV

Client
OpalStar

Industry
Healing Arts, Health, Yoga

Creative firm
Alambre Estudio
Donostia, Spain

Client
Sagardoetxea

Industry
Basque Cider Museum

Creative firm
Fauxkoi Design Company
Minneapolis, MN

Client
The Dollys

Industry
Music

Creative firm
Refinery Design Company
Dubuque, IA

Client
Specialized Bikes

Industry
Entertainment

"The type looks suitably New Age in that vaguely Eastern way that is suitable for a healing center. Gullible hipsters sign up here—bring your own dream catcher."

 "This intriguing image inspires several feelings and takes the mind on a quick little voyage. Good things for a spiritually conscious company.

"The dimensionalized type draws you beyond and suggests a journey to wonderful places. The custom type treatment is both appropriately quirky and very distinct."

 "The dimensionality of the star is exceptional. The type treatment is risky and novel.

"I wish that the type's and star's forms had more in common. Given this star, it is hard to see what is right with these lettershapes. If you are going to make custom letterforms, by all means, do things that unite them with their image."

 "The crisp, clear use of the repeat stripes and the negative shape forming a structural roof says much with very little effort. These elements create a staccato energy and suggest a place, like the mark, that is more than first meets the eye. That's probably just what a logo for a cider museum in Spain should be suggesting!"

 "The Basque Cider Museum would be a great assignment: lots of unique attributes (Basque culture + apples + museums) to play with.

"This image is not altogether clear. The Basque region, straddling the Pyrenees Mountains in northern Spain and southern France, is shaped like a wide triangle, and I suppose the brown rectangles could be Spain squeezing in from either side.

"By the way, in Basque, which is a non-Indo European language, sagar (apple) + ardo (wine) = sagardo (cider). Does the use of a third color for 'herri baten erroak' make it too special for its own good?"

 "Dollys is on its way to being way cool. The added weight of a thicker cast shadow would help the mass of the logo, as would an out-of-register print look. The rope is campy-cool but could be improved by being less detailed and more varied in weight. The 'the' is almost completely lost.

"The color choice and washed-out look are key to holding it together and giving it the unpretentiousness that makes it work."

 "Nice thinking! Classic iconography of country music, circa 1960. The rope's inconsistencies aren't quite rough enough to look like it's this way on purpose. This would be a killer if a length of real rope had been shaped and photographed and slugged in."

 "Unlike some of the other cartoon icons here, this drawing exhibits a stylistic unity due to consistent line variation and style. Nicely executed, and an original, left-field but still relevant idea to boot. I especially like the way the cycling helmet doubles up as an apple-impact protector."

 "Nice quick read with motion and an expressive face. The use of an extreme perspective really helps with the idea of falling, gravity, and speed."

 "Excellent use of speed lines to double as exclamation marks as our hero is about to get bonked by falling fruit."

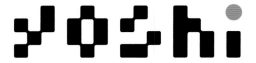

Creative firm
Lloyds Graphics Design, Ltd.
Blenheim, New Zealand

Client
Spark Events

Industry
Event Creation

RH "This logo has a nice color choice; it is well matched tonally."

RM "Simple execution that is well balanced and communicates confidence and competency. The kerning in 'SPARK' needs a little more attention, but the overall effect is a logo that communicates 'This is a company prepared to add ideas and execute on the promises it makes.' "

AW "Handsome, clean relationships. Great color combination: gray plus a color is always a terrific pairing that shows restraint, sophistication, and energy.

"I just checked: Google lists over two million images of sparks, a few of which might be more distinctive than this Illustrator-created version."

Creative firm
Fresh Oil
Pawtucket, RI

Client
Yoshi

Industry
Restaurant

RH "The 'S' remains readable despite the level of abstraction and the unusual name."

RM "This is a clever and expressive logo; it says 'Japanese with a twist.' And it's highly memorable and effortless in its simplicity. Reversed out (on a chef's uniform or on a neon sign), it can't be ruined or weakened. And it's very ownable, too."

AW "Excellent combination of highly abstract digital type—much of which comes from Japan—and the traditional 'Rising Sun.' "

Creative firm
Misha Birmele Designer Graphics
Pasadena, CA

Client
Tharn Theatre Company

Industry
Entertainment

MC "Tharn it! I love the eye illustration here; it's very creepy and powerful, but the type really lets the symbol down. This feels like the designer needed to get off the computer and use his fingers."

RH "The expanse of black and the crop of the eyes definitely communicates an edgy intensity. There is a mismatch between the roughness of the type, the roughness of the black panel, and the roughness of the eyes.

"This logo would have more cohesion if the art had been prepared with traditional cut-and-paste methods using real typewriter type enlarged on a copier or PMT camera, then assembled, copied a few more times for added grit, then scanned and saved as a TIFF for final art."

RM "The eyes peering out of the black window set a bold tone and stark drama. The overall effect of this mark is successful, but attention to craftsmanship and detailing could have turned a solid idea into an enduring one.

"The square form that contains the eyes takes on the shape of a 'blockhead' and makes me wonder if a different shape and possibly including some of the type with that carrier shape would be stronger."

AW "Intensity comes through loud and clear. The scratchy type is well matched to the style of the artwork. Two thoughts on the type: the lowercase 'o' stands out because it is the only miniscule letter (the rule for making something effectively disappear is to have it agree with its surroundings); and the scratchy typewriter type would be even more powerful had it been crafted from an actual antique typewriter, not typeset from a font (note: the 'T's, 'H's, and 'A's all have the same gashes).

"A workaround to finding your own typewriter is to go in and adjust individual characters so each looks unique, and therefore, authentic."

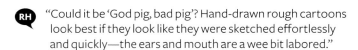

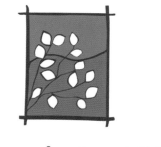

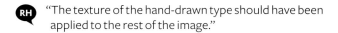

Creative firm
Jeff Fisher LogoMotives
Portland, OR

Client
Good Pig, Bad Pig

Industry
Greeting Card, Retail

RH "Could it be 'God pig, bad pig'? Hand-drawn rough cartoons look best if they look like they were sketched effortlessly and quickly—the ears and mouth are a wee bit labored."

AW "This is how to use vernacular lettering. A delightful solution for a greeting card company."

Creative firm
Alambre Estudio
Donostia, Spain

Client
Lizarrusti Hostel

Industry
Accomodation

RH "The texture of the hand-drawn type should have been applied to the rest of the image."

AW "Charmingly friendly and inviting—perfect for a hostel. Do the positions of the white leaves represent anything (like 'LP,' for example), or are they randomly placed?"

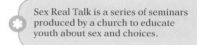

Creative firm
Misha Birmele Designer Graphics
Pasadena, CA

Client
The Russians/Krazy Kieth Records

Industry
Music

The Russians are a rock band from the Pacific Northwest area of the U.S.

Creative firm
KFR Communications, LLC
New Egypt, NJ

Client
Sex Real Talk

Industry
Education

Sex Real Talk is a series of seminars produced by a church to educate youth about sex and choices.

 "Doesn't anyone use their fingers anymore? This would have been much better if it were hand drawn instead of auto-traced in Adobe Illustrator. A little authentic grunge from the handwork, and a bit of texture would give this logo a lot more power and authenticity."

 "Type as imagery is always a good direction for a mark because it forces a degree of abstraction on the proceedings. I thought this was a tiger at first—maybe because the letterforms look like stripes, maybe because the stars suggest a performing animal. But it is almost certainly supposed to be a Russian bear.

"Logos are such finite creations that every element must be carefully weighted. The stars add a clownishness to this mark, which may well perfectly describe the music of this band. If not, perhaps the stars should be downplayed or deleted."

 "Very nice and, again, no reference to church or religion, giving this organization credibility with its target audience. Sometimes it's what you don't show that speaks the most in a logo."

Creative firm
The Marcom Group
Walnut Creek, CA

Client
Sequoia Equities

Industry
Real Estate

Creative firm
The Marcom Group
Walnut Creek, CA

Client
Pacifica

Industry
Real Estate

 "Hip, young, and modern are appropriate descriptors of university student housing owners and tenants. Color is used well as an informative tool, and type contrasts look purposeful. The spacing between 'university' and 'village' is too open, given the closeness of the descender of the 'g' and 'TOWERS.' And 'TOWERS' looks a little too narrow if it is supposed to agree with the width of 'village.'"

 "Wonderful 1950s cartoon feel to the illustration. The thickness of the tree trunks' bases is repeated: in the weight of the brown rule across the top, in the optically equivalent spaces between the illustration and the blue box behind 'SIERRA,' and between the blue box behind 'SIERRA' and 'CREST.'

"The two typefaces have nothing in common except their all-caps setting and their overall set width. They do not share color, size, typeface, or letterspacing."

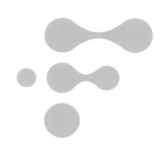

Creative firm
Fusion Advertising
Dallas, TX

Client
Fusion Advertising

Industry
Design

 "This is a good example of a single letterform illustrated to define a product. It's 'fusing' idea is interesting and futuristic and produced very solidly."

 "Fusing employees, clients, and solutions into a single entity is a compelling opportunity. While this is a very handsome logo, does it represent that idea? Because an ad agency sells ideas, abstraction is an especially effective approach in this case. Three into one… how do you show hybridization and process?"

Creative firm
Seesponge
Washington Township, MI

Client
Detroit Creative Directors Council

Industry
Advertising

 "This mark for the creative industry (hence one can get away with more) melds tattoos, automotive sensibilities, and a 'bad boy' image into a strongly vertical mark. I wish the 'the' and the 'th' could be a single type size. They disagree presumably for width similarity. But it is an unecessary complication in an otherwise active mark.

"The texture inside the '30' must be carefully attended: at small repro sizes, it will fill in, so an alternate version must be prepared."

Creative firm
Spark Design
Tempe, AZ

Client
ELEVATION chandler

Industry
Real Estate Development

Creative firm
Fresh Oil
Pawtucket, RI

Client
CHU

Industry
Restaurant

Creative firm
Fresh Oil
Pawtucket, RI

Client
Audio Stop

Industry
Audio, Retail

Creative firm
Firebelly Design
Chicago, IL

Client
FilterOut

Industry
Nonprofit

BIZLOUNGE

RM "This mark establishes a strong, simple standard to identify the entire hotel property. Each time you see a new sign, the system is reinforced and the viewer understands the function, attitude, and style of the place. The logo works alone. I can also see it working well as a series."

AW "Stroke weight is fully used in this mark. A subtle discord exists between the rounded angles in the illustration and the very pointy angles of the letterforms.

"There are three solutions: 'pointy-ize' the artwork, find a rounded version of the typeface you like (many are available with that variation), or simply customize the letterforms you need after converting them to outlines in Illustrator."

AUDIOSTOP

RH "Does this smiley, friendly logo reflect the intended audience? Most people with top-of-the-range car audio systems like to aggressively let the rest of us know about it. That aside, the illustration is well executed. The type is somewhat bland. An italicization of the logo, type, and all would have added some nice forward momentum."

RM "The concept of a sound-propelled car is a winner. The illustration is well executed and color can be distinctively theirs. The typography feels foreign and could use more character."

AW "Sound-as-speed lines is a nice approach. The Isadora Duncan–like smiling driver has a pretty happy car, too."

RH "Nice hand-drawn quality reminiscent of gnarled branches and *Lord of the Rings*–style hippie concept albums. The vectorization of the swirls on either side is somewhat rough and reveals the digital hand too heavily."

RM "A bold, visual nugget that is highly recognizable for a new restaurant. It seems to express qualities of a place that's small, intimate, and personable. The cuisine could be anything since the logo is completely neutral in that way. The handcrafted letterforms must be a part of the character that was desired but could have been crafted and refined further. The design elements on the sides are too detailed for the bold typeface and seem stuck on from someplace else."

AW "Very otherworldly mark for an eatery. Perhaps they specialize in calf's brain in aspic.

"Great that the letters are hand drawn and imported. But notice the relative detail of the curlicues on either side. The letters' bezier points have been reduced so much that equivalent edge quality has been lost. They just look too smooth for such cranky letterforms."

filterout

RH "Simple concept, simply and effectively executed. The red and black color scheme is a no-nonsense choice and reflects the warning message. The stencil effect on the type has been somewhat crudely applied; there are ready-made stencil fonts available that show the finesse of a seasoned designer and should be used in preference."

AW "The simple graphic is tasteful, but I think the type treatment is what makes this a distinctive mark.

"The white lines appear to have been added in studio rather than by the type's original designer. How can I tell? Because the bitty black chips on the 'f' and two 't's look too small."

Creative firm
Jan Sabach Design
Munich, Germany

Client
Perfect Crowd

Industry
Marketing Research

 "The idea of using imagery as letterspaces is unexpected and distinctive. What a great idea. The tutti frutti color scheme actually outshouts the truly distinctive, deserving attribute. It might be a stronger mark in grayscale or simply in black and white."

Creative firm
Smokymirrors.com
Bronx, NY

Client
Len Wallace from The Pulse

Industry
Comic Book News

 "This is a mark-as-diagram. By breaking the dialogue bubble, it uses comic book iconography in a new way. I'd like to see a version in which the weight of the arrow is not bolder than all other lines. A simple logo that has power, so making all lines equivalently weighted is good. However, this contrast in weight creates a focal point, and it may well be the right choice."

Creative firm
Fisticuff Design Company
Orlando, FL

Client
Villains League

Industry
Entertainment

Creative firm
M3 Advertising Design
Las Vegas, NV

Client
Block Sixteen Restaurants

Industry
Development, Restaurant, Nightclubs

 "The smear in the background is what makes this a successful mark. It appears to have been a scan of artwork made off-computer. The 'n-s' ligature is the best bit of type, and because the letterforms are digital versions of what is at heart a hand-drawn Blackletter font, it would be delightful to have adjusted the three very distinctive 'l's so they look more hand drawn.

"I might also tighten the word spacing so the two words relate more to each other (and look like a single unit) than to the left and right edges of the background shape."

 "A restaurant logo for Las Vegas must include diamonds, hearts, spades, and clubs. And... three cherries. The pointy lines from the 's' and 'l' that point to 'ALLEY' are a nice detail. Where do I get this as a tattoo?"

Creative firm
Refinery Design Company
Dubuque, IA

Client
Tri-State Drug Task Force

Industry
Law Enforcement

Creative firm
Reactivity Studio
Austin, TX

Client
Little Leapers Daycare

Industry
Children's Daycare

Creative firm
Gee + Chung Design
San Francisco, CA

Client
DCM

Industry
Venture Capital

Creative firm
Roskelly, Inc.
Portsmouth, RI

Client
East Coast Construction

Industry
Construction

MC "The unsettling juxtaposition of skull and crossbones with the 'Cool Whip' child's face makes you stop and think. I think the mix of gravity and whimsy makes for strong communication in an area where something more serious might be lost in the mush.

"I wish the arched type below the mark was a bit weightier and less spaced. It feels too delicate for the rest of the mark."

RH "Designing logos that need to communicate important issues such as drug-use prevention is one of the most difficult briefs for a designer. It needs to communicate the urgency and seriousness of the message without seeming to, on the one hand celebrate it, and on the other hand trivialize it. While nicely executed, I'm not sure this doesn't resemble a Fisher-Price logo too much; though dealing with children, possibly a more adult, mature logo may have been more appropriate."

MC "I like the frog in diapers, but I wish the illustration was handled a bit more sensitively. The drawing suffers from a bit too much detail and lacks weight and shape relationships that would make it really sing. The type treatment is a bit obvious and cliché."

RH "A humorous concept perfectly attuned to the product—a daycare center. The bouncing type is actually relatively constrained, alternating between just two baselines. Any more would have been overdoing it."

AW "Every type rule is made to be broken when it makes sense to do so. Jiggling the baseline doesn't typically add to legibility, but here it is perfectly applied. Well-used application of color too: 'LEAPERS' naturally belongs with the frog more than 'LITTLE' does."

MC "This is a fun and festive mark. Using the letters is a nice touch to tie the classic Chinese symbol to the client."

RH "Whimsical and unusual."

AW "This is a much more effective way of saying 'DCM [heart] China.' Delightful approach that combines art and type into a single element. The eye seems slightly out of place; its pointiness doesn't agree with the style of the slab serif letterforms, so the overall unity is just a bit affected."

MC "This no-nonsense mark is simple and well crafted—perfect for a construction company. It says 'built strong with no pretensions.'"

RH "I would like to see a version of this logo that only had one stroke thickness."

AW "Figure and ground are used as a resource in this lettermark. Which is in front: the white 'e' or the black 'c'? Proportional stroke thicknesses are well handled, too."

Creative firm
Cirulis
Saint Cloud, MN

Client
Mothers for Breastfeeding

Industry
Breastfeeding

 "The United States of Breasts! Personally, I'd have put the drop of milk directly below the nipple and entirely within the boob. I admire the nice pastelization of the normal flag colors."

Creative firm
M3 Advertising Design
Las Vegas, NV

Client
Rhino Dumps

Industry
Waste Disposal, Construction Clean-up

 "Is this rhino about to unleash his load on us, the viewer? He's certainly pointing in the right direction. Technically, this is a well-executed mark. It is graphic, clean, and powerful, even with the environmentally friendly green color scheme."

 "Too much information. Or lack of subtlety, though it may be appropriate for its waste-hauling market. On the positive side, I love the green highlights in the type. Without them, this mark has two distinct and unrelated parts. 'DUMPS' should be bigger to absorb the letterspacing, which is so big it attracts attention to itself."

Creative firm
Jeff Andrews Design
Salem, OR

Client
Eleventyone Productions

Industry
Entertainment

 "There seems to be three styles fighting here—the rough pen-drawn quality of 'ELEVENTYONE,' the casual vector straightedged quality of the 'E' and the '1,' and the Helvetica afterthought of 'PRODUCTIONS.'

"The overlaying of the elements could be slightly re-fined—there is a sliver of white between the first 'N' and the background 'E' that would disappear if 'ELEVENTYONE' was shifted slightly to the left. Also, the 'Y' needs a little more air between its tail and the extra serif on the lower arm of the background 'E.'"

 "I habitually look for intentional design decisions. This has them in all regards except the choice of font for 'PRODUCTIONS.' The only explanaton is that there must have been a hostage situation in which a miscreant demanded that Helvetica be used somewhere in the mark. If two out of three elements are wiggly, as these are, the different one will stand out. (And 'PRODUCTIONS' is hardly the most important part of this mark.)"

Creative firm
Miller Meiers Design for Communication
Lawrence, KS

Client
Darnell, Inc. of Kansas

Industry
Manufacturing, Marketing, Consulting

 "The 'D' of Darnell in the thought balloon is the core of this concept. And it works. The simplicity of the logo is its strength. To become a more memorable trademark for Darnell, the letter 'D' could be more unique."

 "The dimensionality gives this clichéd bubble idea its character. Now, imagine this as a photo of actual wet drops rather than a digitally-crafted approximation! And it is so easy to do. You could even put a 'D' under the drop, so it gets distorted by the liquid."

ignite a conversation

INVENTIVE
INNOVATIONS

Creative firm
Miller Meiers Design for Communication
Lawrence, KS

Client
H&R Block

Industry
Financial Communications

 "Substituting a message-filled shape for a letterform imposes a degree of abstraction on the legibility of the word. That is generally a very good thing in logo design, where legibility is not nearly as important as attention-getting memorability."

Creative firm
Jeff Kern Design
Springfield, MO

Client
Inventive Innovations

Industry
Inventor

 "This Rube Goldberg-meets-the-Jetsons illustration is a strong icon for invention. If the inventions are highly technical in nature, then this logo could be a tad misleading, but if it's more consumer- or hobbyist-type invention(s), it works. The pastel colors make this less serious and mechanical, which is nice."

 "This diagram mark works just fine. The weak link is the lack of relationship between the image and the type. It would be firmed up by, say, squirting the green rectangle out of the machine, giving a contrast of gray busy shape over green simple rectangle with dropped-out type."

Creative firm
Refinery Design Company
Dubuque, IA

Client
Dubuque Area Chamber of Commerce

Industry
Public Service

 "A key to the city and a stylized compass rose are a fine solution for any Chamber of Commerce. Note: the four stroke weights are all the same. Also, the key's teeth and the arrows on the compass rose match for design unity. I'd love to find a way to make the key into a 'd' for Dubuque."

Creative firm
TOKY Branding + Design
St. Louis, MO

Client
Innovate St. Louis

Industry
Entrepreneur Leadership Program

 "Very nifty use of an 'I' as an illustrative element. The little wedge shapes on the two 'Ns,' the 'A,' and the 'T' add great character. 'ST. LOUIS' seems less resolved."

Creative firm
TOKY Branding + Design
St. Louis, MO

Client
Balke Brown

Industry
Real Estate

 "Handsome and distinctive all-type solution. Best part: the coincidence of the second 'o' and the right edge of the circle."

Creative firm
Korn Design
Boston, MA

Client
Sage Restaurant Group

Industry
Restaurant

 "Too little air between 'CORNER' and the other words (we'd need more on the right as it abuts the 'O,' less on the left due to the space inside the 'E'). I'd prefer the tagline in a similar old-style Grotesque Sans instead of the more contemporary font. I'm not sure the green adds anything, and the change in weight and size doesn't.

"For emphasis, change the color, weight, size, position, or font—but not more than one (unless, of course, you're sure it works better that way!)."

 "Baseline contrast and, to a lesser extent, size contrast identify this all-type mark. With all-type marks, the only one relationship is between the type and the space surrounding it—or, looked at the other way, between the space and the letterforms that interrupt it. So every space must be extremely carefully adjusted. Assume every space is 'wrong,' either too big or too small, and adjust it until it is neither too big nor too small. All that is left is 'just right.'

"Now, compared to the letterspacing of the two primary words, is there too much or too little space on either side of 'CORNER'?"

Creative firm
Prototype Design Lab
Toronto, Canada

Client
Caprice

Industry
Furnishings

 "Highly geometric letterforms. Contrast of letterspacing and an absence of wordspacing. Purposeful color use. Nice design ideas. Luxury furnishings? My guess is a lot of chrome and glass."

Creative firm
Ground Zero Graphic Communications
Coral Springs, FL

Client
InfoTouch

Industry
Computer Touch Screen Technology

 "The insertion of the 'i' into the fingerprint is simple and ingenious. While the type area is carefully crafted—its spacing sizing is sensitively handled—I can't help but think three words in three typefaces and three colors creates some complexity that can be reduced. For example, 'CORPORATION' could be in the same font as 'touch,' reducing typefaces by one; 'touch' could be black or orange, reducing colors by one (and reducing competition with the orange 'i' as the focal point); or 'touch' could be set in the Roman version of the type used for 'info.'"

Creative firm
MINE
San Francisco, CA

Client
Omega High Power Rocketry

Industry
Sales, Machinery

RM "A basic retro presentation that is well illustrated and uses a nice rich red."

RH "A rocketry firm—a great client for which to design a logo. This is almost there. There is no real stylistic connection between type and image; black outlines and some perspective on the type would have been entirely appropriate and in keeping with the rocket. I'd like to see more animation in the girl—more kinetic energy, more vavavoom."

AW "Good clean fun. I guess model rocketry is largely a male diversion. Nice illustration. Two caveats: how do the illustration and 'OMEGA' belong together? (What characteristics do they share?) And does the 'OMEGA' symbol on the rocket look like it stylistically belongs on the rocket or is typeset?"

Creative firm
GraFISK Design
Astoria, NY

Client
Lip Theatre Company

Industry
Theater

 "This is a great execution for *Frankenstein*. It's a bit expected, but at least theater patrons will know what to expect. The moldy, gangrene 'green' is a nice gory touch."

 "The swashes on the 'R' and 'I' give these unorthodox letterforms an unexpected distinction. One senses there is something different about this production of *Frankenstein*…"

Creative firm
USA TODAY Brand Marketing
McLean, VA

Client
USA TODAY

Industry
Publishing

 "It's always very hard to incorporate an existing logo into a larger design—ignore the style of the logo, and you'll have a clash; follow its style too precisely, and you have a pastiche with nothing new or exciting to add.

"Here the designer has made it work. Keeping to the same font (Futura) for cohesion, he has played with size and placement for a lively result that has a celebratory air without any of the usual clichés.

"The cyan block of the original logo is mirrored by the red block at top right, and the purple and green colors naturally complete the palette. My only quibble would be that 'ANNIVERSARY' is not set overlapping like 'USA TODAY.'"

 "This mark is too busy, but the challenge of supplementing an existing logo is to make it seem simple. Start by removing the discrepancies between 'TH' and 'ANNIVERSARY.' One abuts the baseline, the other has linespace above. Two sizes and colors. In fact, kill 'ANNIVERSARY' altogether. '25th' says it all.

"A designer knows he has achieved perfection not when there is nothing left to add, but when there is nothing left to take away."

Antoine de Saint-Exupéry

CHAPTER 2
Sleek & Subtle

Understated Designs That Work

Creative firm
Kimberly Hopkins, Design & Illustration
Nottingham, MD

Client
Barefoot Baroque

Industry
Music, Entertainment

Creative firm
Noble and Associates
Springfield, MO

Client
DuPont

Industry
Packaging

Creative firm
Brand Engine
Sausalito, CA

Client
Propello

Industry
Marketing and Branding

Creative firm
Korn Design
Boston, MA

Client
Ritz Carlton Palm Beach

Industry
Restaurant

MC "I love the concept here. The use of musical notation in a novel way communicates simply and quickly. However, the curves are rough and the weights between the clef and the 'toes' could relate a bit better."

RH "A treble clef is an overused musical motif, but here it's given a novel and appropriate twist for 'Barefoot Baroque,' a four-member chamber ensemble performing in the Baltimore/East Coast area. The execution is dynamic and balanced, and the 'toes-as-notes' carries the concept all the way through. The curves on the ball of the foot could be smoother, however."

RM "A nice twist on a musical note that ties into the client's name. This logo has thorough execution, and the varying line weights give a great sense of a footprint."

MC "This logo has a slightly high-tech feeling that gives a slightly pharmaceutical or scientific aspect to the product. The logo is very clean, simple, and well spaced; it makes me want to know more about the product. The half-full 'O' is a very nice touch."

RH "Typographically, the 'L' has been shortened to visually match the positive/negative balance of the rest of the title, but the 'B' should be shortened slightly as well. It's the same width as the 'O,' so it's mathematically 'correct,' but visually it looks wider."

RM "This is a great concept, although I'd prefer the water above the 'O' to have less weight. But nonethess, it is a great logo."

AW "Fine example of integrating type and image into a unified mark. It has the added value of showing process."

MC "This logo is simple, direct, and modern. The propellers are abstract enough to be memorable. The orange one resembles an asterisk, suggesting that there might be more to marketing than meets the eye.

"The type treatment uses a friendly lowercase that helps with the feeling of simplicity."

RH "The propellers look a little like neckties, probably due to the pointed ends. The number and positions of the propellers also evoke dandelion seeds. This may or may not be intentional."

RM "Great type and colors; however, I think the use of the propellers is a bit obvious."

AW "Orange and gray are very good colors in combination: one is bright, the other muted. Depth is added by shading the grays and varying the sizes of the propellers. Note: the spaces between propellers has been made to look equal.

"On the other hand, the letterspacing of 'pro' seems a bit too open in comparison to 'pello.' And it would be interesting to see propeller renderings that add to the personality of the mark, creating design unity, rather than being mere diagrammatic representations. For example, they could echo the peculiar bent ends of the lower-case 'l's."

MC "Simple and understated—this one really works. The balance of black negative space strengthens the simplicity of the design. The length of the 'stirred' elements could be slightly longer, depending on the application size. It's a bit hard to see them as more than just breaks in the type when the logo is small."

RH "The simple ideas are often the strongest. The break in the type suggests cake icing, or sauce on a plate that's had a finger or piece of bread drawn through it. The execution here is perfect—simple, unadorned letterforms that let the idea breathe. To add anything else to this logo would be to spoil it."

RM "A wonderfully clever logo that is simple, zen-like, and visually fun."

AW "As Paul Rand said forty years ago, the simplest letterforms are the most useful for abstraction. News Gothic, designed by Morris Fuller Benton in 1908, gets out of the way of this simple and elegant treatment for a hotel's restaurant."

Creative firm
Chimera Design
St Kilda, Australia

Client
Svarmisk Resort and Spa

Industry
Travel

MC "The clean, monoweight type has a slick, modern feeling well supported by the icon system. The whole makes an extremely consistent statement. I expect lots of spotless tile and soft, white towels."

RH "The repeated use of the 'a' shape gives the different icons a cohesive and related consistency. The colors are repeated in the umlaut, which ties the type and icon together even more. An elegant and well thought out range of marks."

RM "The use of the shapes in the icons that mimic the 'a' in the name is a very clever idea. Finding tie-ins with other elements of a logo are crucial to its success."

AW "This is a fine example of designing a flexible identity system that requires a balance between consistency and variety. The system is unified through consistent typeface, type size, type color, and symbol equivalency. Varying considerations are type length, second color, and symbol. Though 'svärmisk' is a Swedish name (meaning dreamy, romantic), the client is an Australian resort."

CONSERVATORY

LIVE-2-LEARN

a zest for life and learning

Creative firm
Eye Design Studio
Charlotte, NC

Client
Simonini Builders

Industry
Real Estate

RH "Conservative conservatory. The weight of the scrolls on either side is too heavy for the 'C'—they need to be thinned down (or the 'C' emboldened)."

RM "A nice use of typographic elements to create a balanced anchor for the 'C.' Nice color combination gives this logo a sophisticated look."

AW "How to make the most of found parts. Once again, gray, plus a color, produces an elegant color scheme. If you cover the imagery, you may notice spacing inconsistencies in 'CON-SERVATORY,' particularly between 'SERVA,' which looks tighter than the letters on either end. It would be fascinating if this had been done on purpose."

Creative firm
Lloyds Graphics Design, Ltd
Blenheim, New Zealand

Client
Live-2-Learn

Industry
Professional

RH "Memorable and effective. The connotations of freshness and invigoration reflect well on the team-building and motivational courses for businesses and individuals. A lively, humorous approach."

AW "I am a big fan of letterforms crafted from meaningful materials. It makes them eye-catching and memorable. The simplicity of the type creates a clear hierarchy, and 'zest' delivers the punchline for the distinctive primary element."

Creative firm
Addis Creson
Berkeley, CA

Client
Turn

Industry
Online Technology

 "This is a well-executed mark in a fresh and friendly color palette that keeps it from feeling too tech."

 "A folded (i.e., turned) strip of paper is the basis for this logo. The orange and warm gray are fresh, not too corporate and perfectly, tonally balanced.

"Technically, the 'u' should be slightly narrower than the 'n,' as the top left diagonal corner of the 'u' introduces more white interior space and makes the 'u' look wider than the 'n.' The thin white gap between the 't' and the 'u' is an interesting break from the logic of the rest of the design—would readability suffer if it were removed?"

 "This concept of turning angles gets to the heart of this company. Simple and clean. Overall, a great logo."

Creative firm
IE Design + Communications
Hermosa Beach, CA

Client
MelloMar Brasil Biquinis

Industry
Fashion, Apparel, Swimwear

 "This is a perfect solution for a swimwear company—simple and readable with just a little water added. I wish the word 'BRASIL' were either a lighter color or a lighter weight. Otherwise, a nice design."

 "Nice use of a grad that evokes warmth and water, though the wavelike motif under the 'o' does transform it into a 'Q.'"

 "Striking and fun colors. Very appropriate for a swimwear company in Brazil. I would have liked to see 'BRASIL' in a less heavy color."

"The lowercase contrasted with all caps is obviously purposeful. The 'o' gets a little sea wave illustration—a perfect touch for a swimwear maker—which can be interpreted as a cap 'Q' for those who wish to read a tongue twister."

Creative firm
TOKY Branding+Design
St. Louis, MO

Client
Kaufman Broadcast

Industry
Television

MC "The eccentric letterforms used for 'Kaufman' play well with the retro television screen shape and the graphic wave forms in print applications. There's a lot of detail here that may not work well on an interlaced screen though, especially the word 'BROADCAST' and the thin horizontal line."

RH "The television shape in perspective is a classic 50s motif, suggesting technology and the future. The overlaid waves are somewhat complex and may not reproduce well at small sizes, and the Carson/Emigre arbitrary alignments touching and sliced type, although effectively imparting a certain energy and liveliness, will date this mark quickly.

"Typographically, 'Kaufman' has some inelegant and arbitrary additions—small random serifs and a tail on the 'U' that is stylistically unrelated to the other characters. The colors are very effective—again evoking 50s technology."

AW "Echoes of the 1950s and current design sensibilities crash together in this rather active mark, which makes the television broadcasting company look very forward-thinking. This is an unexpectedly fresh solution."

Creative firm
Fresh Oil
Pawtucket, RI

Client
China Sky

Industry
Restaurant

 "Everything about this feels like it was created with the same hand. The letterforms and the illustration have a nice blend of brushstroke calligraphic freedom and clean graphic strength. Beautifully balanced asymmetry, too. Nicely done."

RH "An evocative logo for a restaurant that avoids the usual Chinese lettering clichés. The drawing does, however, look autotraced—a process whereby a drawing is converted into a vector image. This conversion can sometimes give rise to awkward angular shapes when viewed closely."

AW "The letters are almost one with the illustration. Tasty line quality throughout. If the tree were beneath the word space, would it be in a clearer relationship with the type?"

Creative firm
3
Albuquerque, NM

Client
Upaya

Industry
Massage and Healing Center

MC "The hand shapes used here are friendly, well drawn, and configured into a lotus shape that takes advantage of the negative space to communicate more than one message—or is it massage? The feeling is clean and modern without being cold."

RH "Hands and lotus flower elegantly combine in this mark. The appreciation of the symmetry of the negative interior space shows attention to detail."

Creative firm
The Decoder Ring
Austin, TX

Client
Epic Records (Sony BMG) and Modest Mouse, Inc.

Industry
Music

Creative firm
Tim McGrath
Albuquerque, NM

Client
Osuna Nursery

Industry
Nursery

Creative firm
Alambre Estudio
Donostia, USA

Client
Art Estilistas

Industry
Hair Salon

Creative firm
Michael Patrick Partners
Palo Alto, CA

Client
OurStory

Industry
Online Social Networking

MC "The balance of tension and humor here is great. It's well drawn, too. It makes me nervous wondering which will win—the balloon or the anchor?"

RH "An intriguing visual dilemma."

RM "Nice and simple. I enjoy the two seemingly different objects living as one."

AW "This is a visual contradiction in terms—an oxymoron. Lighter than air meets heavier than water. It appears to have used antique engravings pieced together. Augment this idea with the artistic principle that a lot of muted color is visually equivalent to a little bright color, and the balloon might be gray and the anchor a brighter purple."

MC "The elegance of this mark is in its balance of weights and beautifully drawn curves. Using the counter of the 'O' as the seed with the curving shape of the sprout is both accurate and beautiful."

RH "A well-executed logo that has an appreciation of white space. The shoot, rising from a seed, doubles as the initial 'O' with the seed as the counter. The slightly italicized slant imparts a lightness of touch and an indication of vibrant life."

AW "There is depth and dimensionality to this big 'O,' and thanks must be given to the intelligent and sensitive use of white space. Excellent proportions and craft, too."

MC "The lettering here is very nice, but the ligature between the 'r' and 't' could be a touch smoother. I love the balance of negative space, but I wish the grass was more elegantly handled. The vector shapes are too thin at the tops where the outlines overlap, and too repetitive."

RH "The colors are unusual for a hair salon, and avoiding the 'beauty parlor' pink and purple clichés is to be applauded. The grass/hair idea is novel, though the grass shows its origins as a piece of vector graphics a bit too obviously—some blades repeat themselves. A reversed, 'contrasty' photograph might have given the grass more life."

AW "'Art Stylists,' a Spanish hair salon, uses what looks like lawn grass to indicate hair. There is plenty of empty space, which indicates quality and sensitivity to art principles. The period after the name, spaced slightly out to the right so it doesn't look typeset, gives the brand emphatic resonance."

MC "While the imagery here isn't groundbreakingly original, it does get where it needs to go to communicate the concept. My only quibble is with the spine alignment on the book illustration. Why don't the green and blue pages meet at the bottom as well as the top?"

RH "Two somewhat obvious motifs—a book and a road—are successfully combined using a combination of transparency and color. The customized Optima type aligns with the curve of the road.

"The pages of the book strangely don't meet at the spine, though this may not be important and indeed may add clarity."

AW "This mark is for an online story and picture-sharing site. The transparent book with roadway is more interesting than the type, but they do align along the diagonal edge of the 'y.'"

Creative firm
Sommese Design
Port Matilda, PA

Client
Lauth Development

Industry
Time Share Community

Creative firm
Wonder Worker
Konya, Turkey

Client
Ayhas

Industry
Construction, Architecture

RH "A classic monogram, beautifully executed."

AW "This mark is not right out of the box. It is a handsome combination of 'S' and 'H' whose negative space and positive shape relationships have been given equal loving attention."

RH "Another tree/house combination, this time not for an estate agent or realtor, but for a company that produces wooden cottages for the gardens under the brand WoodenHouse. This logo is much more refined and resolved than other tree/house logos I've seen. Not an original idea, but a nice, balanced execution showing a keen awareness of negative and positive space, nonetheless.

"The font looks handmade. A close look reveals the junctions of strokes are too choked and heavy and need thinning. The 's' is lumpy and uneven, and the letterspacing is all over the place—the distances between the 'u' and 's,' and the 's' and 'e,' are far wider than they should be. However, the 'n' sits directly below the door/trunk, which is a nice piece of finessing. Overall, this logo is a curious mix of polished design and naive clunkiness."

RM "The use of negative space that creates the roof of the house is perfect. The tree symbolizing where the wood comes from is spot on. Ratio of type to icon could use a little finessing."

Pepperland

Creative firm
Dale Harris
Bendigo, Australia

Client
Pepperland

Industry
Entertainment

 "It's great to see well-crafted lettering that is strong enough to stand alone without an icon. These eccentric letterforms have enough character and originality to stand all by themselves. The repetition of shape and consistency of weight in the basic letters allow the use of an occasional swash to add surprise."

"Careful repetition of the ball serifs and the curved bowls gives this logo its lyrical flow."

"An energetic and playful type solution. The enlarging of the third 'p' is a pleasant surprise and adds to the well-crafted typography."

"I am unfamiliar with this display typeface, and it may have been custom lettered for the client. In any case, it certainly doesn't look typeset, and that is the point.

"The swashes are immediately noticeable, but it is the ball serifs, the 'p's' descenders that all hang at different lengths and the 'l's' and 'd's' ascenders that poke up at different heights that create the sense of playfulness that gives this mark character."

Creative firm
Espial
Johannesburg, South Africa

Client
Impande

Industry
Entertainment

MC "This is a beautifully drawn symbol that evokes the goals of the company wonderfully. The typography has clearly not had the same amount of attention as the illustration to which it's married. It feels like all the designer's attention went into the tree/root image, and the type was set in the computer and never touched again. Just a few subtle adjustments to weight, spacing, and scale could have made the type as beautiful as the rest of the logo."

RH "Fine attention has been paid to the stroke widths in this logo, resulting in a harmonious balance between positive and negative space. The bowing of the central bar suggests an egg, a container in which the tree/root system sits—or even a shield.

"As the designer points out: 'Nourishment is symbolically extracted from the African soil by the roots and in so doing, feeds the tree and its branches, which also symbolically resemble roots. The implication being that value may be derived from an African context but then reinvested in order to make the next harvest possible.' A conceptually sound and well-executed logo."

RM "A great concept not fully realized. Some more attention could have been given to the weight of the container in relationship to the 'roots.' A hierarchy in elements would have taken this from a good logo to a great one."

AW "The word 'IMPANDE' means 'root' in Zulu. I love that the horizontal bar gently swells in the middle—only enough to not be parallel at the top and bottom. This is one mark in which I wouldn't change a thing."

Creative firm
CHSC design
Luenen, Germany

Client
Julius Baer

Industry
Financial Institue

 "A nice use of type to create a unique shape. Green is a great color choice for a bank."

 "Very tasteful and reserved, as befits a bank's identity. But this has the added benefit of a customized 'J' and 'R,' giving this mark character. The designer's statement indicates the illustration is a rotation of the lowercase letter 'b,' but to me, that is only incidental to its beauty. Excellent use of a single color: dark green plus a tint of itself."

Creative firm
Admarc Southwest
Midland, TX

Client
Robin Rutherford

Industry
Dental

 "Restful and clean, cosmetic colors—allied with a gray for the type—make this a winning logo. The tooth, with it's embedded heart, and the round, friendly exaggeration of the shapes add to the warmth."

 "The use of transparent colors to create a heart shape is a perfect way to relay that you will feel at ease with this dentist."

 "An abstraction of a tooth is far better than a mere picture of a tooth—especially when there's a heart embedded. The typeface is a humanist sans serif, meaning it is loosely based on handwritten letterforms, so it has a subtle warmth that other sans serifs lack."

HI FI FOR HUMANS

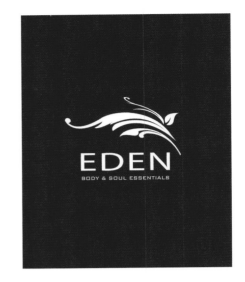

Creative firm
Nei Design Studio
Seattle, WA

Client
Tune Hi Fi

Industry
Music Systems Sales

Creative firm
Dale Harris
Bendigo, Australia

Client
SASI Marketing/Eden

Industry
Health, Beauty

 "The bird's shape mimics the 'u' and 'n' of 'tune.' Eras seems to be a strange choice of font for the byline—here it has been 'uprighted,' as its true form is an italic. Using Futura throughout would have been more consistent.

"A bird as a symbol of a good tune is a good choice. An open beak would have emphasized this connection further."

 "A cute idea. The bird is a great representation of 'tune.' This is a feel-good solution."

 "Design unity is realized through the repeated use of form in the illustration and the letterforms of the primary word. Sophisticated color use in gray plus a bright color."

 "The floral motif has been distorted to give it its flow and grace, and the simple upright type complements this well. The use of Bank Gothic for the byline adds another face—it may have been more elegant to use the same face throughout."

 "Very nice proportions revealed in the contrast of the organic illustration and the constrained type. Emphasis goes to the illustration because of the type's simplicity. In a hierarchy, one element dominates only if the others are purposefully made to be subordinate. That relationship is clearly made here."

GUERNSEY NIGHTCLUBS LTD

Creative firm
Major Minor
Sacramento, CA

Client
Mase Center

Industry
Education

Creative firm
Offshore International Advertising
St Peter Port, UK

Client
Guernsey Nightclubs, Ltd.

Industry
Entertainment

 "A perfect execution for the client. Approach is right on. The atom is a great icon to represent science. The subtle colors and transparency give this mark its modern feel."

 "A combination of a 'G' and a vinyl record's grooves. A neat idea, although the grooves would have looked better if they were thinner and the linework thicker, and if the linework and the font had more cohesion."

 "This mark, for a college's math and science center, reminds those of us who used a Spirograph of the geometric drawings (technically hypotrochoids and epitrochoids) it would produce with its gears and interchangeable pieces. This atom's four electron paths represent the center's four departments."

"The concept of a vinyl record as the 'G' gets to the essence of the company. The typography could have been stronger, but it's a great idea."

Creative firm
Dotzero Design
Portland, OR

Client
Self Promotion

Industry
Film

Creative firm
Brand Engine
Sausalito, CA

Client
Sugar Bowl Bakery

Industry
Bakery

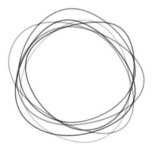

Creative firm
Goodform Design
Brooklyn, NY

Client
Mulberry Acupuncture

Industry
Holistic Medicine

Creative firm
CHSC Design
Luenen, Germany

Client
Club Zero

Industry
Entertainment

MC "The two symmetrical letters in this monogram are a gift the designer used wisely. There are a few lumpy curves which, if fixed, would elevate this logo to media heaven."

RH "An elegant monogram that interestingly achieves a vertical balance by being backslanted."

Mulberry Acupuncture

MC "This looks like the designer let the computer choose the type. Unrelated fonts can work, but they almost always need to be chosen with care and redrawn to make the weights and spacing relate. This didn't happen here.

"The mandala symbol is appropriate, but it's also calling for a more beautifully drawn 'M,' and a few other elements that relate to it in weight."

RH "A questionable use of two stylistically different fonts. The concentric circles suggest acupuncture points, and the floral arrangement suggests calm and natural well-being. But the lopsided symmetry of the flower, the way the repeated 'M's are not all aligned with the circle inside them, and the poor letterspacing make this logo a bit unresolved."

RM "The colors used in this logo are very calming, which is smart, because many people get anxious when they think of acupuncture. I enjoy how the 'M' was used in the icon and carried to the type. Great execution."

AW "Love the illustration, with the initial 'M' repeated as an ornamental motif, and the pink needle marks. But I cannot recommend the contrasting initial caps in the typesetting beneath. The problem is that the initials are less potent letterforms than the lowercase characters, so an imbalance is created. Which is more important, the comparatively dull initials or the comparatively lively lowercase characters? Mixing quirky types, as these two are, is very risky.

"In addition, the spacing after the 'M' is much greater than after the 'A,' and the 'A' seems too high off the baseline."

MC "The S-B ligature is so well done I almost missed it! The type is a very sensitive balance of size, weight, and spacing, and it all blends well with the several other elements in the logo. The chef's hat 'S' is a nice touch."

RH "The use of dark brown instead of black in this logo adds warmth. The bridge is also reminiscent of a baker's apron. Maybe more could have been made of this, possibly by positioning the hat above where a head might be. The 'S-B' ligature is well executed."

RM "This logo makes me hungry. The color combination gives a great sense of what the product may taste like. The 'S' in the baker's cap is a nice touch, and the type is sound. Great logo."

RH "The bright transparent rings evoke glow sticks, wristbands, and intertwining rubber bands. Energetic, lively, and fun. Typographically, the font would look better if the strokes were the same width as the linework above."

RM "The intersecting shapes and their vibrant colors give this mark the energy it needs to represent this client properly."

AW "Reminds me of the liquid-filled glowing tubes kids wear as bracelets and the rubber bracelets made popular by Lance Armstrong's LiveStrong campaign. Both excellent references for a night club event aimed at young people."

H&R BLOCK
PARTNERS
SERIES

Creative firm
Miller Meiers Design for Communication
Lawrence, KS

Client
H&R Block

Industry
Financial, Tax Preparation

 "Conceptually, this is a very nice mark, suggesting communication and agreement, although the weight and style of type used for 'PARTNERS SERIES' could relate better to the digital feeling of the speech bubbles.

"From a marketing and positioning standpoint, it looks a lot like the Charles Schwab 'Talk to Chuck' campaign. This could confuse consumers and make H&R Block seem like more of a follower than a leader."

 "Overlapping speech balloons effectively illustrates communication and partnership—like a Venn diagram, we're both discussing the same thing, here represented by the green square. The gray and black color scheme does look somewhat gloomy and corporate.

"Typographically, we have a mix of condensed and non-condensed Frutiger. The stroke widths have been kept uniform, adding to the cohesion, though strangely the leading (interline spacing) varies."

 "This is a variation on the existing corporate mark. The green square has had dialogue bubbles added, and the Frutiger Bold typeface has had a condensed version added.

"Now, what if one bubble had the black flush left 'H&R BLOCK' speaking, and the other bubble had the gray flush right 'PARTNERS SERIES' speaking? Just one typeface and one size, with color and position adjusted for contrast. This would enhance the relationship between image and type, so every visual thread is woven into irreducible cloth."

SEVEN

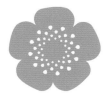

EngenderHealth
for a better life

Creative firm
5Seven
San Francisco, CA

Client
Self Promotion

Industry
Design

 "There are several very successful things all working together to make this logo work. Choice of type—mixing the serif '5' with the sans serif letters—adds both form and weight contrast to emphasize the double read. The use of color supports the type contrast.

"The open letterspacing also contributes to the double read by allowing the '5-S' to read both as a letter and a number. Overall, a very deft solution that demonstrates this design firm's skills."

 "The combination of sans monoline and a more flowing, serif '5' makes for an interesting combination. The orange and gray are tonally expertly balanced as well."

"Wow, a great type solution; it's so simple and effective. I'd hire this design firm with that kind of unique thinking."

 "Lovely abstraction of a '5' and 'S,' taking the key parts of each to create a new character. I believe the 'V' has been customized with their diagonal stroke ends, giving the mark just a hint more individuality."

Creative firm
BBMG
New York, NY

Client
EngenderHealth

Industry
Philanthropy

"The logotype feels very comfortable with the flower icon. The flower as a metaphor is a simple, lighthearted choice that suggests health without being too literal. The choice of fonts for the tagline is unfortunate. Keeping the san serif consistent would have worked better."

"Aligning the flower (a symbol of growth and health) with the left of 'Health' and 'for' would add more elegance, as would designing the stamens on a five-fold symmetry to reflect the arrangement of the petals. The fonts are a very poor mismatch. Using Syntax throughout, but altering the color or the size, would give more cohesion."

"You have me all the way until the tagline. The shapes in the flower and the typeface used in 'Engender,' particularly the 'g,' are terrific. But why that serif face for the tagline? The sans serif (Syntax) is a slightly condensed Humanist; the serif (Cantoria) is quite round. The lowercase 'e's' crossbars don't match the primary type's.

"How much better this might have been had the small type been set in Syntax Light. Or select a Humanist typeface that is available as a sans serif and a serif, like Thesis, Rotis, or Officina. Remember: design is about removing unnecessary complexity."

PLAZA ATHENEE
H O T E L

Creative firm
Paragon Marketing Communications
Salmiya, Kuwait

Client
Plaza Athenee

Industry
Hospitality

 MC "The design of the mark here is elegantly suggestive of art nouveau design, a choice that nicely supports the name of the hotel.

"Two things let this logo down a bit: the first is color—the garish red seems out of place in this elegant setting; the second is the extremely poor letterspacing. If both things were corrected, this logo would better live up to its elegant positioning."

RH " 'PLAZA' is too airy compared to 'ATHENEE.' Closing up the letterspacing would add finesse and evenness to this otherwise elegant mark."

RM "Great care was given to letterspacing. Combined with the elegant illustration, this is a winner."

AW "Very tasteful mark throughout. It has had all complexities removed so the result seems inevitable. There is no question that luxe quality is to be found at this establishment."

Creative firm
Moby Dick Warszawa
Warsaw, Poland

Client
Polish Security Printing Works (PWPW)

Industry
Finance

RH "A traditional, sober mark evocative of engraving for a traditional printer. The bolder diagonal strokes of the 'W's have been carefully aligned. This does, however, introduce an overall backward slant to the whole design."

AW "This logo, for the company responsible for printing Polish zloty, shows the letters 'PWPW,' which stands for 'Polish Security Printing Works.' Being part of the financial industry, the company must appear conservative and trustworthy, so basing the design on printers' marks from the 1500s and 1600s is an informed decision.

"A nod to modern times is in the slight jog of the inverted 'P-W' pairing; this would have been quite difficult in the days of metal type where kerning required filing away the metal block on which the raised letterforms were molded."

Creative firm
Tomko Design
Phoenix, AZ

Client
Pantheon Development Partners, LLC

Industry
Custom Building

 "This logo is smartly designed and beautifully balanced. Using the 'O' inside a concentric circle to represent the famous hole in the dome is a smartly abstract choice that is tastefully continued by the curved 'H.'"

"The secondary type is placed to make the circle perfectly centered—carrying the Roman ideals of symmetry and balance into the twenty-first century. A tweak to the letterspacing by tightening up the 'P-A' and opening the 'H-E' would make this logo perfect enough to get even Emperor Hadrian's approval!"

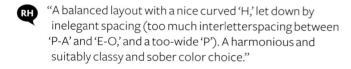 "A balanced layout with a nice curved 'H,' let down by inelegant spacing (too much interletterspacing between 'P-A' and 'E-O,' and a too-wide 'P'). A harmonious and suitably classy and sober color choice."

"The 'O' of 'PANTHEON' is centered, but what distinguishes this mark is the curved stroke of the 'H.' Note that the two lines of secondary type ('DEVELOPMENT PARTNERS, LLC') are sized and positioned to match the cap height of the primary type."

Creative firm
Tomko Design
Phoenix, AZ

Client
Il Cortile

Industry
Multi-use Development

 "This is a very nice, unexpected approach for an Italian-themed development. While the choice of serif caps nods (somewhat predictably) to Roman type design, the 'whimsyness' of the border takes us somewhere new and makes the logo feel modern and fresh."

 "Great playfulness in the border. The shapes and their varying sizes work well together. I would have liked to see 'THE COURTYARD' not stated twice."

 "Centering the type in an enclosed space is a logical and descriptive handling of a Phoenix development featuring an Italianate piazza. The colors are harmonious because the dark green is a shade of the light green; black has been added."

Creative firm
Guarino Graphics & Design Studio
East Northport, NY

Client
D&F Development

Industry
Real Estate

Creative firm
Turner Duckworth
San Francisco, CA

Client
Oakville Grocery

Industry
Grocery Store

Creative firm
Ryan Paul Design
Brooklyn, NY

Client
Aquila Property Company

Industry
Real Estate, Sports

Creative firm
19Blossom
Singapore

Client
Self Promotion

Industry
Creative

MC "The tree here is quite beautiful, but it feels small in proportion to the type. I also wonder why it wasn't flipped horizontally to help fill in the space on the right so that the word 'MANOR' didn't have to be spaced so much more openly than 'LOCUST.'"

RH "The wider spacing of 'MANOR' to match 'LOCUST' is a somewhat awkward design solution. Centering the two words above one another might have avoided this. Interesting and unusual color choice."

AW "Beautiful tree rendering, with legitimate interpretation of a locust tree. Second-best feature is the flip-flopped use of blue. 'MANOR' has been spaced out to match the overall width of 'LOCUST,' so there should be a bit more space between the tree stem and the 'M' for optical consistency."

MC "This mark has a very nice double read, with the fox face and leaves both rendered beautifully. Balancing the modern mark with a traditional, large-and-small cap serif type creates a nice tension that seems appropriate for a golf club."

RH "A simple, elegant, and conservative solution that brings class and style. There is an unfortunate resemblance to two faces, black and green, facing outward from the center. They look like they have bulging foreheads, glum expressions and *Simpsons'*-style overbites. Making the 'cheek fur' of the fox more pointed would remove this distraction."

RM "A nice use of positive and negative space to create the fox's face, added with classic type, makes this logo refreshingly solid."

AW "The fox is inherited from previous branding, but the styling and revisualization is very well done. This slightly abstract rendition of foliage is far more appealing than a direct illustration of trees."

MC "The rabbit illustration here has an inviting storybook nostalgia to it, reminiscent of Beatrix Potter's *Peter Rabbit*.

"The choice of cap and lowercase serif works perfectly to support the friendly, vintage feeling. The clean simplicity of the rendering style gives the whole thing a charming, wholesome, and friendly feeling."

RH "A friendly, approachable logo that promises a friendly, approachable shopping experience. The temptation is to go for an overtly traditional 'heritage' design approach, but this manages to be contemporary and fun."

RM "Great execution and concept. The simplicity of the illustration adds to the effectiveness of the overall mark. This logo is visually fun and expressive."

AW "The stylized bunny looking in the picnic basket: friendly and descriptive of discovering goodies within. Note the subtle use of negative space infiltrating the top edge of the basket. Century Old Style is a familiar typeface and adds significantly to the trustworthiness of the brand."

MC "The blossom, reminiscent of Japanese heraldic emblems, is beautifully rendered but way out of scale to the type. The old-style numbers, treated as letters, need a bit more weight to balance the caps, but otherwise, it's a nice choice of type for the symbol."

RH "The heavy flower overwhelms the delicate type. Reversing the type out of a rectangle might be an effective alternative. The white strokes of the letters would then mirror the finer white lines in the central part of the flower."

RM "This is a striking and weighty logo. Type is being crushed by the weight of the flower. Perhaps a bolder typeface could have been used."

AW "These numerals are treated as letterforms by virtue of the 'missing' word space. The outermost curves of the flower echo the organic shapes of this particular typeface."

Creative firm
Yiying Design
New South Wales, Australia

Client
Kinetoscope Pictures

Industry
Entertainment

 "This logo for a St. Louis–based digital film and video production house, which specializes in high-definition video production, uses a typographic effect reminiscent of overexposed film.

"The finer elements of the letterforms have been blown out. This works more successfully on some letters than others—the addition of the clipped uprights on the 'S's' and the retention of the fine strokes on the 'C's seem arbitrary. Replacing the 'O's with film reels is somewhat obvious and perhaps unnecessary."

 "The type is a little overwhelming. The use of film reels as the 'O's is clever. Overall, this is a memorable logo."

Creative firm
Burçin Ünver
Istanbul, Turkey

Client
Nakkas Miniature Arts

Industry
Design

 "This handsome mark demonstrates a sensitive balance of detail to empty white space, but the type—a spider's web of swashes—doesn't relate to the mark at all."

 "While there is a cohesion between the swooping circular swashes of the type and the circular design of the flower motif, the execution is overly complex. Lines overlap lines in the type, producing a mass of unresolved detail at odds with the simpler motif above."

C R O S S I N G S

WOODSON COMMUNITY

Creative firm
Robison Creative Studios
Springfield, MO

Client
Crossings Church

Industry
Religion

 "Love the arrow pointing upward in the negative space of this mark for a church. Interesting branding of a church that looks nothing at all like a religious entity. But the same can be said of any mark that doesn't indicate its product or service."

Creative firm
Reactivity Studio
Austin, TX

Client
Woodson Community

Industry
Subdivision Community

 "The gradation suggests a misty morning. A conservative, but not dull logo."

 "This mark is for a subdivision near a significant pier. Terrific use of asymmetry; that the letterform 'pier' is off to the right suggests attachment to shore. At any rate, we can tell the left edge ends in space. Maybe the gap in the 'W' in 'WOODSON' should have been closed so it agreed with the illustration."

Creative firm
Open Creative Group
Birmingham, AL

Client
Blue Room SalonSpa

Industry
Spa

Creative firm
Ground Zero Graphic Communications
Coral Springs, FL

Client
Artemis Consulting

Industry
Business Consultant

 "Very nice color choice of powder blue and brown makes this a mark reminiscent of vintage perfume labeling. Typographically, the square television shapes in the condensed weight of Microgramma (used on 'THE' and 'SALON SPA') is perhaps too futuristic a choice here. The dotted lines show their computer origins a wee bit too heavily. Maybe a more finessed or even a hand-drawn approach would have given the whole mark more cohesion."

 "The whimsical feel and color combination really make this mark sing."

 "Stylish color combination and classic typography make this mark hit its target. Are those spit curls?"

 "In Greek mythology, Artemis was the daughter of Zeus and Leto, and the twin sister of Apollo. She was usually depicted as the maiden goddess of the hunt, bearing a bow and arrow. Having said that, there isn't anything particularly feminine about this interpretation of her, so 'strength' and 'power' are evidently being emphasized.

"Excellent repeated element in the illustration and primary type. Ancient letterforms are a great idea here, but these Roman characters (Trajan, digitally expanded) really might have been Greek-inspired instead (Matthew Carter's 'Sophia' comes to mind)."

Creative firm
KRUSE
London, UK

Client
Highgrove Homes

Industry
Property Developer

 "It's the old 'word-spacing-bigger-than-the-line-spacing' thing again…"

 "This logo's flower illustration is a great nod to the name of the community. Its flowing in and out of the block has a nice energy."

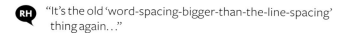 "Elegant color combination: gray plus green and a tint of the green. Given the spacing of the illustration and 'AXMINSTER,' I think 'THE GROVE' has too much word spacing. Either enlarge 'THE GROVE' or—better yet—open the letter spacing within it to absorb the space. Axminster, by the way, is a village near the River Axe in southwestern England."

Creative firm
KRUSE
London, UK

Client
Provincial & Western Homes

Industry
Property Developer

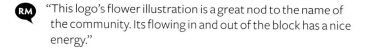 "A very clean and simple approach. The serif type says 'classic and strong.'"

"This monochromatic mark succeeds because of its use of off-centered negative space and the contrast between the rectilinearity of Chichester Cathedral's profile and the semi-circular 'sky.' Chichester is famous for its cathedral, which dates to 1076."

Creative firm
Robison Creative Studios
Springfield, MO

Client
New Life Church

Industry
Religion

Creative firm
Robison Creative Studios
Springfield, MO

Client
James River Assembly

Industry
Religion

Creative firm
IE Design + Communications
Hermosa Beach, CA

Client
Silverhook Alaska Coffee

Industry
Coffee

Creative firm
IE Design + Communications
Hermosa Beach, CA

Client
MGM Grand Hotel & Casino Centrifuge Bar

Industry
Restaurant

 "Whoever said 'God is in the details' must have been a designer. This logo is almost there but needs a touch of the divine when it comes to letterspacing and weight.

"The space between the cap 'L' and the 'I' needs to be tighter; possibly reducing the length of the base of the 'L' would help. The same is true for the space between the 'F' and 'E.' The cap 'N' is much too heavy for the rest of the logo, and the 'L' and 'E' could use a bit of a diet as well. Using a lighter value of green for the leaves helps to reduce their visual weight and creates a nice asymmetry and movement in the center."

 "I love the clever gesture in this logo, but the calligraphic lettering needs some subtle improvements. Giving the 'J' the same variation in thick and thin as the 'r' would emphasize the fish and balance the slightly bottom-heavy design. The placement of the 'ames' feels a bit too close to the 'r,' and 'iver' needs a ligature to make it balance."

 "Aha, but if it didn't have an eye, we'd probably not notice there was a fish! The 'ames' is too close to the 'r' of 'river.' Moving the line up would improve the white/black balance. I feel the large 'r' is also too heavy. Though it's a 'capital' at the beginning of a word and so it may be due more emphasis, the 'J' should match."

 "Simple and clever. The type is well executed. Notice how the thins and thicks within the font are perfectly placed."

 "This illustration skillfully incorporates several images into a wonderful whole. The type is a nicely selected mix that works well together, too. My only (very tiny) quibble is the overly thin and clean keyline around the art. Why doesn't it relate to one of the other two lines in weight and treatment?"

 "That's not just a dot. It's an eye, and it helps us notice the fish in the 'J-R' ligature, essential to this mark for a church. I wonder whether the mark would have greater dignity if the fish shape were to exist without the eye."

 "A nice idea well executed. The distressing on this logo has been applied more evenly and thus realistically than would be the case if a pre-distressed font had been used, as is the case in some of the other logos we've seen. The fine keyline seems to have escaped the ravages, however.

"The colors are coffee colors, which is entirely appropriate, and the blue is a nice, harmonious counterpoint. The handle of the mug could be bigger, which would help the concept."

CENTRIFUGE

 "While this logo is technically accomplished, I wish there were more motion in the design."

 "A nice inversion of the 'G' in the font—Glaser and Caruso's Avant Garde—gives us an 'e.' Shame the last 'e' is an 'E.' Maybe the 'e-G' combination at the end would have looked overdone."

"Coffee steam as a glacier as an initial 'S.' Brilliant. Now, why does 'ALASKA' have greater prominence than 'SILVER-HOOK'? Because, of the three words (each in a different typeface, by the way), 'ALASKA' alone is tan, so its difference indicates specialness.

"If, for example, 'SILVERHOOK' were blue at the same time, all three words would have their own unique color—and the whole would be made better—or just louder, which isn't necessarily the same thing."

"This reminds us that letterforms are malleable and interpretable: an 'e' is an inverted 'G'! To make this novel invention visible, the blue 'I' and cap 'E' need to go away, which raises the question: is the 'e-G' relationship worth it? There are two good ideas—the 'e-G' relationship and the blue 'I'/illustration—in conflict in this one mark."

Creative firm
Prototype Design Lab
Toronto, Canada

Client
Atelier

Industry
Social Entertainment

 "The graceful curves of the 'A' on this logo seem to come to a screeching halt when they run into the leafy Victorian goober that seems to have appeared from an unrelated dingbat source book. And the far too light and open type is being overwhelmed by the larger and heavier strokes of the 'A.' "

 "An interesting decorative treatment for the 'A' evokes the baroque exclusivity of a private lounge. The curves on the black element need smoothing, and the type is too fine and too close to the rest of the logo—the 'R' especially relates by proximity more to the black element than to the rest of the word."

 "A nice use of shapes to create the 'A' icon. I would have liked to see this logo all one color or just the type in black."

Creative firm
Zafari, Inc.
Mount Pleasant, SC

Client
The Wrenn Group

Industry
Residential and Commercial Development

 "A tree must be the image most overused in development logos. Although this tree is certainly a cliché, at least it's been given a bit of a twist by adding the bird and the eccentric swirls.

"I do wish that the rough texture of the tree and the type were a better match. The type feels over-distressed; a slightly bolder treatment with a matching rough edge would have tied things together a bit more."

 "The chunky roughness of the tree—obviously a piece of clip art—sits uncomfortably with the finer texture of the type and the finesse of the 'grass' and the bird. A collision of unrelated parts."

 "Great colors. The subtleness of the wren is a nice surprise. It is nice how it interacts with the rest of the mark."

Creative firm
Cottos Design Group
Woodstock, GA

Client
Fulton & Kozak

Industry
Financial

MC "This logo has a wonderful mix of buttoned-down seriousness and goofy friendliness. The loopy forms of the ampersand contrast with the predictable and rather staid type treatment to make it seem like these are two guys in suits who might actually have fun working together."

RH "Sober without being dull, this logo for a financial institution manages to say very little, but at the same time, it conveys 'reliable,' 'classic,' and 'not too stuffy.'"

RM "Typographically sound. The use of color gives dominance to the ampersand. A very solid logo."

AW "The ampersand is an infinitely interesting and beautiful character, and it has been since its invention as a shorthand for 'et' (meaning 'and') in 63 BC. What a tasteful contrast between fluid and formal, bright and muted, and vertical and horizontal."

Creative firm
Mary Hutchison Design, LLC
Seattle, WA

Client
Innovative Beverage Concepts, Inc.

Industry
Beverages

MC "This logo suggests a high-tech company with advanced engineering and design capabilities—all with two circles and one line. Whether they're cans, or cups, or coffee rings left on the table (the specific interpretation is left to the viewer), the absolute reductionism of this logo is an example of how well minimalism can work."

RH "In logos as simple as this, especially ones without any text, the 'TM' takes on almost iconic importance. Its positioning must be considered as carefully as any other element.

"A simple logo reminiscent of Bauhaus typography in color and shape, though its meaning remains ambiguous—what does it represent, if anything?"

RM "A minimal approach. The circles bubbling up, representing liquid, is a nice idea."

AW "Simple, evocative shapes suggest thought bubbles and containers."

Creative firm
Unreal
Baton Rouge, LA

Client
Advertising Federation of Greater Baton Rouge

Industry
Nonprofit Industry Club

Creative firm
Cirulis
Saint Cloud, MN

Client
Self Promotion

Industry
Design, Illustration

Creative firm
Donatelli & Associates
Hillsboro, OR

Client
Columbia College Student Housing

Industry
Housing

Creative firm
Dustin Commer
Wichita, KS

Client
American Diabetes

Industry
Nonprofit

RH "Liquor and vinyl—a great combination. Technically, the 'BIZZARE BAZAAR' text is too fine, the 'y' of 'Vinyl' is too close to the edge of the cartouche, and the background pattern is subtle almost to the point of invisibility."

RM "A playful logo for a fun event. The type selection really carries this logo and gives it its whimsical feel. Perfect, giving the viewer a sense of what to expect if the name did not already raise an eyebrow."

AW "Great fun. Slight sense of depth from the drop shadow. The ampersand is not quite resolved, as it doesn't belong with either 'LIQUOR' or 'Vinyl' and isn't worthy of being particularly noticeable at all. To make it go away, make it agree with something. Maybe the sans serif used in 'BIZARRE BAZAAR'?"

MC "This is sooo close to great. If the bird were drawn with a bit more grace to match the swashes on the branch, and the branch were actually an intentional monogram, this lark would really sing."

RM "Great use of negative space around the illustration. I would like to have seen the diamond shape with some of the rough lines around its border that the illustration carries. A simple and effective mark."

AW "A personal mark for an illustrator whose name, Cirulis, means 'lark.' Is that a 'C' and 'S' hanging from the branch?"

MC "This is a nicely designed and executed mark with tastefully spaced type, but why is it a flower made of trees—if that's what they are?"

RH "Are those trees? The green color certainly suggests that they are, but they also look like petals in shape. Either way, this logo suggests a green and pleasant campus that is a far cry from the concrete modernism of the college accommodations I'm more familiar with. The off-white Futura and its letterspacing effectively matches the negative/positive balance of the tree/petal shapes."

AW "Excellent depth. Scale and color make this mark sing. Bigger and brighter look near; smaller and darker look far away."

MC "While this is a well-executed symbol, its optimism verges a bit too much on the comic and childlike to feel like a strong position for a diabetes nonprofit."

RH "A happy dancing figure is now almost de rigueur when designing a logo for an organization dealing with a life-threatening illness. Though optimistically looking to the positive is, of course, what many involved need to project, you may be forgiven for thinking this was for a pep pill or dance class instead.

"Having said that, this is still a nicely executed logo combining a flower and a figure that cleverly unites four limbs (plus a head) and five petals seamlessly."

Creative firm
Zumablue!
Westlake Village, CA

Client
Designer Lighting

Industry
Lighting

 "Unlike many logo designs, this logo has a good reason for its decorative ornament. Hanging the well-spaced serif type on a decorative bracket is both smart and amusing. The white inline in the ornament is a bit too thin to work successfully at small sizes and is unnecessary to the concept; but otherwise, this logo hangs together well."

 "What makes this a handsome mark is the typographic alignment and contrasting free-form organic shape that hints at hardware for a wall-hung lamp."

Creative firm
IE Design + Communications
Hermosa Beach, CA

Client
Opticard

Industry
Professional Services

 "Bringing down the dots so the 'i-dot' aligns with the top of the 'O' and the ascender of the 'd' would add elegance, as would extending the descender of the 'p' to the baseline of 'PAYMENT.'"

 "With this logo, color is used to connect the illustration and type. The dark blue dot on the 'i' becomes the bottom left dot in the illustration, which shares its light blue color with the secondary type.

"The word space between 'PAYMENT' and 'SERVICES' is equivalent to the space between the 'p' and 'PAYMENT,' and it should be closed up a bit so the two words in the phrase relate just a little more to each other than to the word above."

MARKET PLACE

A MODERN CLASSIC

Creative firm
Underscore
London, UK

Client
Warner Estate

Industry
Retail

MC "Good design is often little more than combining the right elements in an interesting way. This logo is a great example. The choice of vintage clip art ghosted behind a classic, period serif font makes this modern take on Victorian design completely appropriate for a shopping center."

RH "A harmonious choice of type (Engraver's) and image. The type itself is very nearly centered; a lucky coincidence places the symmetrical 'T' in the center, and a nudge to the right would position it perfectly. The background is possibly too complex to have type happily laid across it."

RM "This is a great illustration, although it may be too elaborate depending on applications. The contrasting tones create hierarchy. The type is very tasteful and well set."

AW "If this looks British, it is deserved. The artwork for this mark, representing a refurbished retail center in Bolton, near Manchester, England, is extracted from a Victorian wallpaper pattern, and the type is a variation—of which there are many—of engraver's type. The gray and black coloration is also of the period. A fine example of capturing an era appropriately."

Creative firm
Organic Grid
Philadelphia, PA

Client
Messaging Online

Industry
Technology

 "An old idea, but techinically well executed."

 "Rings and swooshes were a rage in the 1990s, especially for Internet companies. What makes this one interesting is its use of negative space."

Creative firm
M3 Advertising Design
Las Vegas, NV

Client
Floral 2000

Industry
Floral Shop and Boutique

 "Although intriguing, this logo bears the signature complexity arrived at by repeated use of scaling and flipping functions. There are areas of overlapping elements that are overly complicated and need handwork and refinement. Close examination also shows that the symmetry is not precise."

 "Elegant and tasteful. I enjoy how the thick and thin line weights interact and hint to a flower."

 "Overlapping typographic elements create an impression of a flower for a very high-end Las Vegas floral boutique. Colors usually associated with babies lend a warm familiarity."

Creative firm
5Seven
San Francisco, CA

Client
Amalfi Coast Music Festival and Institute

Industry
Nonprofit

Creative firm
Christopher Design
Cleveland, OH

Client
Clean Air Conservancy

Industry
Environmental, Nonprofit

 "A nice congruence of shapes—domed cathedrals and violins—serves as the basis of this logo, bringing together location and performance. It's a shame that '& Institute' are both on one line, breaking the one-word-per-line arrangement. It might have worked better to use 'and' and to drop 'Institute' down one line, possibly arranging the type on the same baseline as the dome.

"The 'f' of 'festival' is disconnected from the rest of the word and, although readable, might have benefited from being closer or even drawn as a more flowing shape, breaking continuity with the typeface to be more like the 'f'-shaped hole on the actual instrument."

 "The idea of overlapping silhouettes that express specific location (the dome of Vietri sul Mare's Church of San Giovanni Battista) and subject (classical music as represented by a violin) is enhanced by doubling the duty of the violin's 'f' hole. This bridges* the illustration to the type, though there is arguably too much space separating 'f' and 'estival.'"

*Pun intended.

 "The type (Trajan again—a popular choice!) is too weak; the bolder weight would have been more effective. The fan/gust-of-wind motif is clearly portrayed, though the spirals more resemble 'e's than 'c's. "

 "Clouds and wind surrounded by type, in the color of the sky on an ideal day. Very tasteful.

"A tip o' the hat to Trajan, whose use rights I'm beginning to wish I owned! If typefaces were clothing (which they are in their way), logos are being much too frequently dressed in the exact same button-down shirt. There isn't enough distinction in that for your clients, so either choose a less-used face, or do something to the existing letterforms to make it your—and your client's—own."

JUDEL · VROLIJK & CO.

Creative firm
Braue: Strategic Brand Design
Bremerhaven, Germany

Client
Judel · Vrolijk & Co. Design & Engineering GmbH

Industry
Yacht Design

 "This is a very gracefully drawn swordfish illustration that fits well with the strong-but-elegant serif type. The swordfish-as-metaphor aptly expresses the speed and strength of a seaworthy yacht slicing through the waves."

 "The fineness of some of the elements in the fish is at odds with the thicker serifs of the type. A refined logo, both in color use (blue/gray is a classic conservative color choice denoting masculinity and tradition) and in the letterspaced type."

Creative firm
Braue: Strategic Brand Design
Bremerhaven, Germany

Client
Gothmann Optik

Industry
Eyecare

 "The lowercase 'g'-as-glasses gives a twist of humor to an otherwise rather stern logotype. The letterspacing of the primary type is very nice, but the space between the words underneath is far too open."

 "The eyeglass 'g' is here used as just that—eyeglasses. The unicase type (mixed upper and lowercase) ensures there are no ascenders to break up the rectangular layout. Again, the word spacing is greater than the leading; increasing the point size of the tagline would allow the space to be closed up and the baseline to align with the bottom of the 'g.'"

Creative firm
Kendall Ross Brand Development & Design
Seattle, WA

Client
Sahale Snacks

Industry
Snack Foods

 RH "Those little 'TM's sure add to a designer's grief."

 AW "Lovely. The leaf-as-lightbulb is refreshing. Now, just custom dent the repeat letterforms so they look truly and properly aged and not like letters in a pre-damaged typeface."

Creative firm
Crave, Inc
Boca Raton, FL

Client
Beyond Intelligence Group

Industry
Retail, Bake Shop

RH "I'm unsure as to the meaning/relevance of the smiling character at the bottom—the sunburst and wavy hair are almost nautical. The shape of the 'frame' is reminiscent of the label on the neck of a bottle—again, is this a relevant connotation for this logo of a bakeshop to be evoking?"

RM "A nice shape to contain this playful and energetic illustration. I can see this making great signage for the front of a retail shop."

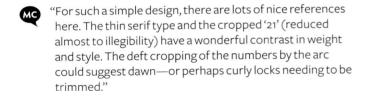

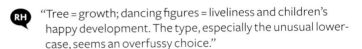

Creative firm
A3 Design
Charlotte, NC

Client
Planet 21 Salon

Industry
Hair Salon

MC "For such a simple design, there are lots of nice references here. The thin serif type and the cropped '21' (reduced almost to illegibility) have a wonderful contrast in weight and style. The deft cropping of the numbers by the arc could suggest dawn—or perhaps curly locks needing to be trimmed."

RH "The crescent cropping the number effectively portrays a planet without recourse to an emblem resembling Saturn…"

RM "The arc and the type rising out of it give a great sense of the sun rising and a new hair day beginning."

AW "Neutral type permits greater abstraction while retaining its legibility. This minimal illustration conveys 'planet' without unnecessary decoration."

Creative firm
Aijalon
Lincoln, NE

Client
Dimensions Foundation

Industry
Educational

RH "Tree = growth; dancing figures = liveliness and children's happy development. The type, especially the unusual lower-case, seems an overfussy choice."

AW "This semi-serif typeface was well chosen to relate to the many pointy ends of the curves in the illustration. If 'DIMENSIONS' had been brown, it wouldn't 'belong' to only one figure, and more importantly, the dancing figures would stand out more in their joyful growth."

Creative firm
Zafari, Inc.
Mount Pleasant, SC

Client
The Wrenn Group

Industry
Commerical, Residential

 "Aside from the fact that this is yet another tree, it is headed in a nice direction. The color and basic design here are quite nice; the details of the illustration and type, however, need some work.

"The use of Adobe Illustrator's spiral tool is all too evident. A good tool should be an aid to creating a good design more easily, not a limit that prevents further development. These spirals need to be adjusted in weight and their ends tapered slightly to echo the beautiful curves in the tree trunk.

"The mix of cap and lowercase in the lettering has weight issues, as well as some spacing problems. The 'o' and 'e' are much too heavy for the cap 'B', 'W,' and 'N,' and the 'o-W-e' spacing needs to be tighter."

 "The curves belie the hand-drawn style of this logo. The spirals meet at clunky angles, and the light touch of a pen or brush may have been more appropriate here. The colors are effectively used to emphasize the small bird; by using the same color as the type, the eye is drawn to it despite its size."

 "One way of creating design unity is to create limited palettes: of colors, typefaces, sizes, and line weights. This ensures similarities. The colors used in this mark are related by all having been desaturated (by adding white). The line weights are all equal to the thin strokes of the letterforms. The result is a mark that looks purposeful and the result of a plan."

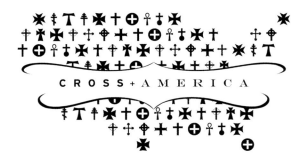

Creative firm
James Marsh Design
Hythe, Kent, UK

Client
Avril Allen

Industry
Coaching

Creative firm
Gouthier Design
New York, NY

Client
CADA (Christian Art & Design Association)

Industry
Nonprofit

Creative firm
Kendall Ross Brand Development & Design
Seattle, WA

Client
The Bellevue Collection

Industry
Retail Centers

Creative Firm
TOKY Branding+Design
St. Louis, MO

Client
Compton Gate

Industry
Real Estate

MC "With the optimism of a children's book and the warmth of a Christmas toy, this charming illustration has just the right qualities for a therapist. It's one of the smartest logos I've seen."

RH "This has what many other logos lack—an idea. This idea is unusually rendered as a full-on illustration. This handmade quality suggests a hands-on personal company approach that a cleaner, more corporate logo would have lost. Entirely appropriate and unique."

RM "This is a great illustration and concept. The ropes waving backward give the viewers a sense that this bird is flying on his or her own for the first time."

AW "Fantastic symbolism for a personal coach and therapist. Handsomely realized."

THE BELLEVUE
COLLECTION

MC "The elegance of the mark and the type design are compromised by the far-too-open letterspacing. Tighter spacing and a slight increase in the size of the mark would make this sophisticated design a winner."

RH "Nice color choice—olive drab and black. The letterspacing is bigger then the line spacing, a no-no that should be avoided (unless, of course, it's your big concept)."

RM "The intersecting lines of the flower represent the collective quite nicely. Great color combination and finely executed type."

AW "Gorgeous image and color, but what strikes me is the subtle customization of the letterforms and the counterintuitive emphasis on 'COLLECTION' rather than 'BELLEVUE.'"

MC "The 'dingbat' cross pattern filling the continent balances well with the mixed typefaces inside the brackets and does a great job of representing the diversity of Christians as well as the diversity of design styles. The tiny cross between the words is unnecessary and distracting though. It makes me want to read it as 'Cross plus America' or 'Cross and America.'"

RH "The multitude of crosses represents the multitude of designers and their individual styles, all, however, coming together under their common uniting banner as Christians. The implied white area between the braces creates a clean space for the type, again a combination of old and new, sans and serif (Interstate and Engravers)."

AW "The multitude of styles shown in the crosses is consciously brought out in the two very different typefaces used in the primary type. The ornamental swashes, separating the foreground from the patterned background, are curvy and thus necessarily crop off the underlying characters. This helps define its position in the foreground. Pity that individual crosses repeat. If each were unique, the 'manyness' of the samples would seem infinite."

MC "This logo is well balanced and extremely legible considering the level of ornamentation. There are a few lumps in the curves at the top, but otherwise, this is a well-considered design."

RH "An appropriate logo for a condo development—classy, conservative, and elegant. It manages to be original as well, with a nice wrought-iron concept and a stacked type arrangement where the type touches rules top and bottom. Only the free-floating chevrons on either side of 'GATE' let it down conceptually."

RM "This is a strong logo in many ways. The iron filigree and the play off of the client's name is very clever. Also, the type weights and face are used very appropriately."

AW "Wrought iron handsomely approximated. The proportions look so right that I expect image research was used wisely."

133

Creative firm
Timber Design Company
Indianapolis, IN

Client
Service Warehouse Corporation

Industry
Grocery Warehousing and Distribution

MC "This logo has a wonderful mix of type and color. The shapes are well thought out, and the type fits comfortably within them. The word 'Service' is beautifully lettered, and even the comstock works well. The retro styling creates a warm, friendly, and nostalgic feeling."

RH "A beautifully executed retro logo. The stroke weights are consistent, the colors are balanced and appropriate, and the wings and stars are classic motifs of the period. It's almost too well designed—take a look at the originals this design takes as its inspiration, and you'll often find the idiosyncrasies of hand-drawn type and uneven manufacture."

RM "I am instantly drawn to this mark because of its great execution and retro stylings. Since it conveys a sense of heritage from this company, I am thrown off by 'SINCE 1995.'"

AW "A beautiful re-examination of 1940s and 1950s roadside signage. Add a little rust around the edges, and this would be a vintage porcelain enamel sign."

Creative firm
Niedermeier Design
Seattle, WA

Client
Sara's Massage

Industry
Massage

 "There's a nice, casual delicacy to this logo. The hand-drawn lines are nicely echoed by the choice of type. It would be great if this used hand-drawn letters instead of a typeface, but if you've got to use a typeface, this one's well chosen. The weak spot here is really the hands; a little variation of the weight of the lines would tie them in better with the rest of the elements."

 "A hand-drawn approach for a hands-on client. It's touchy-feely, friendly, and the colors—pink and brown—are very appropriate."

 "Healing hands. The old-fashioned style illustration gives the sense that this therapist will take good care of you like mom may have."

 "I can feel the benefit of Sara's magic hands in this touchy-feely wiggly mark. Now, just adjust repeat letterforms to make it look less like a font and more like hand lettering. (Or actually hand-letter it—we can all make funky wiggly letters for our clients who need them—and ensure their unique and proprietary use!)"

Creative firm
Rhonda Harshfield Design
Louisville, KY

Client
Studio 151

Industry
Beauty

 "A lock of hair as an 'S,' echoed by the 'S' in 'STUDIO.' The letterspaced condensed type is a shorthand for 'sophisticated,' but may be seen as somewhat dated.

"The letterspacing on 'STUDIO' and '151' should be equal, and the 'HAIR & NAIL SALON' looks a little like an afterthought. (It bears no stylistic relation to the rest of the design.)"

 "The hair forming the 'S' is what drew me to this logo. I like how the top of the 'S' starts to form the head from where the hair is coming.

"The type could be stronger on 'HAIR & NAIL SALON,' but overall, this is a strong logo."

Creative firm
Lloyds Graphics Design, Ltd.
Blenheim, New Zealand

Client
The Deli

Industry
Food and Produce

The Deli is a specialist, premium-quality delicatessan that operates in the same premises as The Living Room, a café/restaurant offering fine cuisine in restrained, elegant surroundings.

RH "Typographically, some air between the 'l' and the 'i' and more between the 'D' and the 'e' would help. I'd be tempted to bring the 'THE' down between the 'D' and the 'l,' aligning the top of it with the top of the 'l' and centering it in the space—not centered on the logo as a whole. Though less logical, it may look more elegant."

RM "Here is a great logo that complements the main venue, The Living Room. Both logos have similar stylings but work great together or on their own."

AW "Lovely interpretation of Italian art deco style. This mark does add value to the represented business. Simplify this—and make it even more elegant—by reducing 'THE' to match 'AT THE LIVING ROOM,' and equalize spaces in 'Deli': move the 'e' over to the right and open the space between the 'l-i' pairing."

Creative firm
Spark Design
Tempe, AZ

Client
ELEVATION chandler

Industry
Real Estate Development

 This logo was created for a deli within a hotel.

 MC "The exuberant sprout is a strong anchoring element in this logo. The type is well chosen for its small x-height and tall cap height. The contrast gives a feeling of energy to the type that might otherwise be overshadowed by the colorful liveliness of the icon."

 AW "This mark for a resort's delicatessen is fresh, clean, and healthy. It shows how important spacing can be to the character of a mark."

Creative firm
Spark Design
Tempe, AZ

Client
ELEVATION chandler

Industry
Real Estate Development

 RH "Letterspaced Gill looks very 80s, very 'New Romantic record sleeve trying to evoke an English classicism'—but maybe that's just me and I'm too close to design trends to see it as a non-designer would.

"There isn't really an idea at work here—just a playful letter-form. The curves on the right corner of the 'e' are somewhat lumpy, and I wonder if something more closely related to the font below would have been more harmonious."

AW "The customization of this letter 'e' shows great sensitivity to form because it looks right. The rhythmic red over gray is another nice touch."

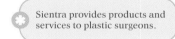

Creative firm
Eye Design Studio
Charlotte, NC

Client
Rhein Medall & Simonini Builders

Industry
Residential, Real Estate

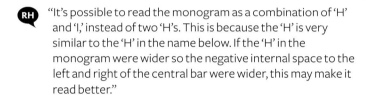 "It's possible to read the monogram as a combination of 'H' and 'I,' instead of two 'H's. This is because the 'H' is very similar to the 'H' in the name below. If the 'H' in the monogram were wider so the negative internal space to the left and right of the central bar were wider, this may make it read better."

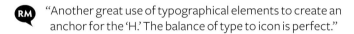 "Another great use of typographical elements to create an anchor for the 'H.' The balance of type to icon is perfect."

Creative firm
Michael Patrick Partners
Palo Alto, CA

Client
Sientra Medical

Industry
Medical Devices

 Sientra provides products and services to plastic surgeons.

"Plastic surgery is a difficult business to successfully project in a logo—too literal an approach may be off-putting—but maybe this design goes too far the other way and is too abstract. An interesting execution in search of an idea."

"The two identical shapes creating the 's' is a clever idea. The feel of this logo is perfect for its client—corporate, yet modern."

"Magnificent use of negative space in this mark for products and services to plastic surgeons. The type is a semi-serif face, so named because it has swells that hint at serifs at the ends of strokes. The colors seem arbitrary, but perhaps they are the only ones not being used by competitors, or they are inherited from an earlier identity program."

FURNACE
FILMS

Creative firm
Rule29
Geneva, IL

Client
Furnace Films

Industry
Entertainment

 "A very nice monogram treatment that is almost there. The positive/negative inline effect on the 'F' alludes to Blackletter types and adds a gothic touch.

"Technically, the curves need a bit of smoothing, and 'FILMS' appears too bold. This is because the two weights of Trajan have been used, but 'FILMS' is too large. Reducing it would bring the stroke widths into line with 'FURNACE.'"

 "The flaming 'F' is a great idea that has not been successfully executed. A little more finessing is needed to get it just right, but a strong concept nonetheless."

"An 'F' rendered with style as flames. Does the typeface Trajan, based on letters carved into a column in 114 AD, make any particular sense here? It is certainly an elegant typeface, but it does have its own baggage of meaning. Either way, does the increased boldness of 'FILMS' add to or detract from the potential elegance of this mark?"

Creative firm
Richard Zeid Design
Evanston, IL

Client
Asparagus

Industry
Restaurant

 "The curved asparagus icon in this logo is quite nice. I am less enthusiastic about the choice of type. The purple color is great, but the curved shapes of the condensed serif are at odds with the curves in the icon. A bit more integration would make these two elements relate better."

"Wonderful Asian feeling to the asparagus heads in this mark for a French/Vietnamese restaurant in Indiana. Perhaps the French spelling would have been too foreign: *asperge,* with the asparaguses around the central 'e.'"

Creative firm
TwoByTwo
Mahwah, NJ

Client
Share & Care

Industry
Nonprofit

 "Very nice symbolism of a hug. The ampersand looks a little small, because its top doesn't quite reach the waistline (top of the x-height). The 'are' in 'Share' and the 'are' in 'Care' are not spaced exactly the same. Is one more perfect than the other? And if so, why isn't the lesser one matching it? Nitpicks such as this separate pretty good from excellent."

Creative firm
Ginger Griffin Marketing and Design
Cornelius, NC

Client
Loopy Line Design

Industry
Custom Embroidery

 "The rabbit has jumped through the loops, an elegant touch. The rabbit itself looks a wee bit stationary—a more lively and active jumping pose would have added even more life to the charming illustration."

"A wonderful illustration that really captures the essence of the client's business."

"A mark for children's embroidery, so the motion line behind the bunny is really a snapshot of stitching. Very nice. The word 'line,' though properly typeset, looks more open than 'loopy,' so some customization should have been inflicted."

Creative firm
Wolken Communications
Seattle, WA

Client
Avec Amis

Industry
Event Planning

 "Closer examination reveals that the cartouche surrounding 'events' is enlarged (compare to the one above), but 'events' still seems too tightly enclosed.

"There are some strange curves in the capitals, especially on the thicker strokes of the 'V' and the 'M,' that are probably intentional but unfortunately resemble autotracing artifacts."

 "Great combination of rough illustration and type. They complement each other very well. The balance of elements brings this logo together."

 "Compare this to the Market Place mark (on page 123). They both mine the same design territory and use equivalent parts. And both are symmetrical, which gives them a shared formality. But this mark uses a quirkier typeface and contrasts all caps with arched lowercase."

Creative firm
Jacob Tyler Creative Group
San Diego, CA

Client
Vastardis Capital Services

Industry
Investment

 "Again, the 'word-space-bigger-than-the-leading' issue appears … The combination of Roman Trajan with that essentially modern face, Alessandro Butti and Aldo Novarese's Microgramma, makes for an unusual and not entirely successful combination."

 "Customizing a familiar face, like Trajan, is a great way to make it the client's own. The brown dots are essential to unifying the two lines of type. The only other attribute they share is an optically equal line width. The word space is too open."

360°modern™

Creative firm
Wolken Communications
Seattle, WA

Client
360 modern

Industry
Real Estate

 "Fresh, modern color choice—especially unusual for a real estate agent, where navy blues and serifs would be the norm—but entirely appropriate for this company: a collection of real estate agents that focus on classic and contemporary modern architecture.

"Technically, the degree is too heavy. The lower curve of the 'e' needs to be pulled out to the right to stop the letter looking like it's about to topple forward, and there is too much air between the 'r' and the 'n.'"

 "Great type solution. The differing weights and colors help to distinguish the two parts of this logo."

Creative firm
Prototype Design Lab
Toronto, Canada

Client
Doku15

Industry
Restaurant

 "An interesting and bold approach, though possibly readability has been sacrificed for graphical elegance. The '15' hanging on the tail of the 'K' is a nice piece of detailing. The rounded serifs of the '15,' however, seem to be at a disagreement with the sharper, more pointed gray curves."

 "The stylized type and subtle colors are a perfect match. Gives a feeling of sophistication."

"Abstract letterforms are harder to read, but they are also far more distinctive, as in this mark for a Japanese restaurant. It takes great sensitivity to fashion a 'D,' an 'O,' and a 'U' from the same curved element.

"The brown shapes are problematic because they don't agree with the gray shapes, and neither do they contrast sufficiently. The slab serifs and organic shapes are just a little different than the pointy-ended curves."

Creative firm
Markatos Design
Carlsbad, CA

Client
Bravo Dog Training

Industry
Dog Trainer

Creative firm
Conversant Studios
Hagerstown, MD

Client
Kiran's Sweet World

Industry
Food

Creative firm
TOKY Branding+Design
St. Louis, MO

Client
Butler's Pantry

Industry
Food

Creative firm
Source/inc
Chicago, IL

Client
Dunewood Condominium Association

Industry
Real Estate

"This logo has a nice sense of humor in its updated retro elements. I love the dog illustration, and the allusion to circus imagery feels perfect for a dog trainer.

"The big red type works well with the delicate details in the illustration, but the diagonal white lines filling the letters should be a consistent fill pattern that extends all the way to the edges of the letters rather than stopping just short as they do in several places, like the 'A' and the 'O.' There's a bit too much space between the 'R' and 'A,' and the ornament below 'DOG TRAINING' needs to be simpler or heavier. Other than that, I think this one sits and stays."

 "A simple idea—show the cute, obedient dog! The dog illustration is very nicely executed but let down by the type. The stripey caps are a nice idea, but the white stripes themselves are unevenly and awkwardly spaced and terminate within the letters rather than overlapping them completely.

"The extra flourish at the bottom is too light and unneccessary. Letterspacing 'DOG TRAINING' to match 'est. 1980' would add more cohesion."

 "I love the mix of illustration style and type here. The classic bold square serif perfectly balances the eccentric humor of the illustration. This logo makes it look like a tasty place to eat."

 "A charming and elegant mark that communicates tradition and service without stuffiness. The inky illustration is full of character, in contrast to many logos that are clean and graphic to the point of losing their personality. The blue wash adds interest.

"The only criticism is that the domed plate looks like it's been enlarged—the line weight and character don't fit the figures exactly."

 "This logo uses a very stylized illustration to create a fun feeling for the viewer. It also gives the viewer a sense that this company enjoys what it does."

 "A charming line drawing with a loose wash fill, coupled with types that were in existence in 1966, give credibility to this long-lived purveyor."

 "Sometimes more is more, and a logo for a sweet shop seems like a good place for over-the-top decoration. But when everything screams at the same level, the hierarchy gets lost. The type, especially the word 'WORLD' needs more weight or size or both to compete well with the rest of the art."

 "An interesting use of clip art that could do with more focus and bolder type. The colors are unusual but work."

 "This is just perfect. The choice of no-nonsense serif caps with the delicately graceful grass is a sensitive juxtaposition. Even the choice of colors evokes the location with sophistication."

 "A perfectly executed and balanced logo, making the most of negative space to suggest a cropped scene behind the type—the grass is obscured either by an intervening dune or by an invisible panel around the type.

"The three lonely blades to the far right add just the right amount of randomness and realism. The blades themselves are realistically overlapped without undue complexity and with a sense of balanced crosshatching. Finally, they all lean to the left, suggesting a breeze."

 "Less is more. That statement certainly applies to this logo. A great combination of negative space and type, giving a real sense of place."

 "Negative space—background—becomes visible when it is made to appear in the foreground. The implication here is that 'DUNEWOOD' is on a sign staked in front of the grasses. The neutral typeface allows the grass blades to dominate."

Creative firm
Jacob Tyler Creative Group
San Diego, CA

Client
Cocchia

Industry
Fashion, Apparel, Golf

Creative firm
Braue: Strategic Brand Design
Bremerhaven, Germany

Client
Shin'Sei Chinesische Heilkunst

Industry
Healthcare

 "Conservative. The speedlines of the swing are well constucted, though more of them (three or four) would have added more kinetic movement. The type is possibly a bit fine and weedy.

"'Styles that swing,' and the dual meaning of 'swinging' may be too outre for the golf clothing market, where style is not the first thing that springs to mind. Full marks for not replacing the 'O' with a golf ball."

 "I believe this logo uses the arch of a proper golf swing very nicely and consequently, relays its golf tie-in in the tagline."

 "The hand/leaf symmetry is executed in a refined and consistent manner. The curves on the 'S's are somewhat lumpy, though this could be due to the font rather than the logo designer.

"The curved serifs on the 'H' and the 'N' are too small and look weak next to the other serifs. The rounded ends to the fingers should be echoed in rounded leaf veins and rounded spikes on the letters."

 "Heilkunst is a holistic medicine developed by a German doctor over 200 years ago that emphasizes health and nature. That the primary type has been tweaked to pick up Asian-like letter shapes is logical and convincing."

Creative firm
Braue: Strategic Brand Design
Bremerhaven, Germany

Client
Bernadette Krieger Personal Coaching

Industry
Personal Coaching

RH "Helping/catching/supporting hands. An old idea, but an appropriate one. Nicely drawn."

RM "A great color combination giving dominance and subordinance. The icon is a nice idea of some helping hands getting you to your goal."

Creative firm
Sugarbot Design
Amarillo, TX

Client
Amarillo College Animation Group

Industry
Computer Animation, Graphic Design

RH "The 'a-g' monogram can also be read as a capital 'A'—for Amarillo. If it had been possible to match the line weight of the type below with the tri-line initials, that would have added a further degree of cohesion."

RM "Excellent use of the lines connecting to create the energy of animation. I would have liked to see the word 'animation' be the same value gray as the dark gray of the icon to better relate."

AW "The 'a' and 'g' are drawn in an op art style, then overlapped to create visual motion for a college's computer association. The use of shading is continued in the title, creating harmony between the illustration and the type."

Creative firm
Ellen Bruss Design
Denver, CO

Client
Kent Place

Industry
Real Estate

Creative firm
Fauxkoi Design Company
Minneapolis, MN

Client
Lily Red PR

Industry
Marketing

Creative firm
Yiying Design
New South Wales, Australia

Client
Snail Rabbit Publisher

Industry
Publishing House (Children's)

Creative firm
KFR Communications, LLC
New Egypt, NJ

Client
Cornerstone Calvary Chapel

Industry
Recreation

MC "Updating classical forms can be a challenge, as demonstrated here. The choice of base letterforms is a happy one, and the weight of the vines and rosettes doesn't impede the overall legibility, which could easily have happened.

"Unfortunately, the inconsistent weights and awkward curves of the vines, and the odd placement of the rosettes, ruin the execution of a mark that should have worked."

RH "Almost there. There are loops of vine that seem to vanish and then reappear—for example, under the 'P.' The overall color and negative/positive space is effectively balanced for a mark that portrays upmarket luxury living."

AW "Initially, looks very pretty and well crafted, but oddities reveal themselves: the vines relate to the internal structure of the 'P' much better than to the 'K'; the rosette on the 'P' is integrated with the vines, but the rosette on the 'K' is unattached to anything; one rosette is on a vertical axis and the other is on a diagonal axis; and the vines are drawn to one thickness throughout, except around the 'K.' These unresolved relationships make the mark look unfinished."

RH " 'LILY' and 'RED' have been effectively centered, despite their differing letter counts. 'PR and Marketing' is somewhat small and is tending tó get lost on the patterned background. It would also have been more elegant to use the Bodoni throughout—specifically, the obvious differences between the two capital 'R's jars."

RM "A very fun logo. The patterned background could have been simplified. Using all caps on the entire logo could have made it a bit stronger."

AW "A speech bubble crafted from typographic swashes gives this mark its delightful character. I cannot imagine why two typefaces are necessary to describe the two lines of type though.

"The two attributes the lines of type share are centeredness and horizontal baseline. The five attributes they don't share are: typeface, type size, line width, all caps and caps/lowercase, and color. That's a lot of contrast and precious little unity."

MC "This is a perfect icon for a children's publisher and close to perfect as is. My only quibble is with the ears. I wish they were a bit larger so they'd read a bit more quickly as rabbit's ears when the mark is small. As is, they're almost the size of the expected snail's antennae, so the rabbit half of the mark is the second read."

RH "Details like the tail make this an appropriately friendly mark. The colors, pink and gray, are typical of a product aimed at children, though the pink makes this specifically feminine."

RM "This is a very appropriate icon for this client. It is friendly and inviting, and the color combination adds to the fun factor."

AW "Wonderful idea and fine execution for a children's book publisher. We even get a sense of excitement from the twin exclamation marks."

MC "There are some nice things going on in the rough, hand-drawn quality of the softball and wings portion of this logo. I wish a similar sense of craft had been given to the 'CORNERSTONE' lettering. It looks like a computer font with a computer-generated comstock that lacks the attention to detail of the drawn elements. The same is true of the 'CALVARY CHAPEL' lettering."

RH "Typographically, the mechanical outlining of 'CORNERSTONE' has led to some thin black lines between letters that need looking at. 'CALVARY' is touching the wing on the left, which would be an easy defect to correct."

AW "For a church group, this is a pretty aggressive-looking softball team. In fact, if you cover up the dove, it could easily be a mark for a secular squad. It is so evident that it must be by design."

Creative firm
Becky Nelson Creative
San Diego, CA

Client
Sanctuary Home & Garden

Industry
Home Décor

 "A great combination of sans and serif types. Simple and elegant."

 "Design can be improved far, far more often by removing something rather than by adding something. 'SANCTUARY' is wonderfully visualized, and the 'T' is beautifully crafted. The problem here is the competition between the illustrated 'T' and the ampersand directly beneath it. There is room for only one organic character in this logo, and the 'T' deserves all the attention. The ampersand could be removed entirely: just run 'home garden' beneath 'SANCTUARY.'"

Creative firm
MINE
San Francisco, CA

Client
Yen Jewelry

Industry
Jewelry

 "The simplicity of the logo is its strength. The nature-inspired 'Y' gives the viewer some insight as to what to expect from this jeweler."

 "Very handsome mark for a jewelry designer that introduces expectations of nature-inspired forms. The limited color palette is restrained and very elegant. Is this a 'Y' for 'Yen,' or an eerie yet elegant face? It could be either, depending on how you perceive it."

ST DAVID'S
ACADEMY

Creative firm
Underscore
London, UK

Client
St. David's Academy

Industry
Education

St. David's is a rugby academy in Wales. A stylized 'd' has been rotated seven times to create this symbol.

MC "The choice of red and the pointy tattoo shapes that make up this mark give it a slightly violent, edgy strength that is both modern and timeless. I like the choice of the classic Roman-style serif with this logo; it gives it the authority of a manuscript, although there are a few letterspacing issues that should be addressed."

RH "A celtic/calligraphic hybrid that resembles both a flower and a tattoo. The subtle but noticeable central rugby ball shape echoes the interior spaces of the 'd's.'"

RM "The blood red color is very appropriate. The sharpness of the 'd's also relates the rough nature of the sport. This is a great logo."

AW "Even before reading the designer's statement, I was able to see the seven 'd's that make up this rugby ball for a British school. Why seven? The designer says, 'the seven intelligences of human beings: logic, linguistic, aesthetic, sporting, emotional, social, and spiritual.' Good goals for a school to have.

"Does Trajan have anything to do with Britain, or is it chosen simply because it is elegant? There isn't anything wrong with that, but neither is there anything particularly right with it. Regardless, the space on either side of the apostrophe needs to be closed up."

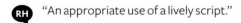
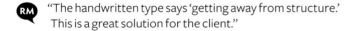

where the living is easy

GrayPoint™

Creative firm
KRUSE
London, UK

Client
escape

Industry
Property Developer

RH "An appropriate use of a lively script."

RM "The handwritten type says 'getting away from structure.' This is a great solution for the client."

Creative firm
Mary Hutchison Design, LLC
Seattle, WA

Client
GrayPoint

Industry
Internet e-commerce

RH "Running two words together and using capitals or a color/ weight change to differentiate them—originally a necessity of Web addresses, but soon adopted to connotate technical forward thinking and modernity—has become very much a cliché in recent years. It has also given rise to some unintentionally hilarious misunderstandings: 'Experts Exchange' was getting traffic that had nothing to do with Web design and programming because of their unhyphenated name, 'expertsexchange,' and 'Powergen Italia' becomes 'powergenitalia.'"

RM "A simple type solution that falls slightly short of perfection. Minor adjustments, and we have a solid mark."

Creative firm
Mary Hutchison Design, LLC
Seattle, WA

Client
Innovative Beverage Concepts, Inc.

Industry
Beverages

 "Great and appropriate color is achieved in this simple but effective logo."

 "Design unity is achieved by using a shape very similar to the 'o' from the type as a frame for the leaf. The familiar typeface here is Eurostile, designed in 1962 by Aldo Novarese. It is a lowercase extension of his 1952 Microgramma, which was originally an all-caps family."

Creative firm
Organic Grid
Philadelphia, PA

Client
Thaddeus Harden Photography

Industry
Photography

 "The inconsistencies are consistently applied—and that's what gives this typographic mark its interest."

 "A great icon and type solution. The mimicking of weights in the icon and type that represent each other is a nice visual connection."

 "The unexpected inconsistencies—the short 'PHOTOGRAPHY,' the even shorter slash—generate all that is special about this mark. And those inconsistencies are compacted into the illustration."

Creative firm
M3 Advertising Design
Las Vegas, NV

Client
Chronos

Industry
Retail, Packaging

MC "This is a nice choice of classic Roman serif applied in a thoroughly modern way. Mixing the serif with the ultra-modern ball-clock motif, and adding all the space, gives this logo a feeling that old is new again—just right for a calendar company that plans to produce designer versions of some of our oldest timekeepers."

RH "The ball-clock motif, reminiscent of a classic, 50s design, is given a kinetic spin by the paler offset version."

RM "Typographically simple. Visually expressive. An excellent use of letterspacing—wide, but appropriate."

AW "A mark for a series of calendars, this illustrates time in the twelve stations and the ghosted repeat in the background. The '3' in the center presumably refers to the designer's name."

Creative firm
Squarehand/ The Buddy Project
Astoria, NY

Client
The Receiver Band for Stunning Models on Display Records

Industry
Indie Music Band

"While at first glance, the Spencerian-style swashes don't seem to relate to the uncial letterforms, the mix works due to some deft positioning of the elements and plays with scale.

"The 'The' is my only critique: a slightly larger 'h' and a slightly lower 'e' would have kept it in better proportion and position."

"The ever-increasing point sizes suggest the volume being turned up. Pink is a very unusual choice here— it contradicts the vigourous swashes and illuminated eccliesastical letterforms. Maybe this reflects contradictions in the music?"

"A mark for a musical band that doesn't use Blackletter! The Receiver, based in Columbus, Ohio, is probably folky— suggested by the Celtic uncials—and a little subversive— suggested by the cacophonous swashes."

Creative firm
Braue: Strategic Brand Design
Bremerhaven, Germany

Client
van der Linden

Industry
Health Care

"While leaping people for healthcare is almost as overused as trees for development companies, this is a very nicely drawn example. The curved forms of the leaf are echoed in the upraised arms, and the gesture is gracefully rendered. The type, too, is well spaced, and the choice of a mixed cap and lowercase serif gives this a friendly, yet sophisticated feeling."

"Another dancing/jumping figure, this time for a wellness company and not a cancer charity. The leaf curves into the figure elegantly, and the 'V' of 'Van' mirrors the edge of the leaf. The italic type is less successful."

"This is a cute idea. I enjoy the energy that the human shape within the leaf exudes. It says 'wellness.' Nicely done."

"Negative space is beautifully used in the illustration. The primary type is an example of a unicameral typeface: it mixes caps and lowercase into a single character set. This requires redrawing the lowercase letters so they are the same weight as the caps. (Incidentally, 'Physiotherapie' is not a typo; it is the German spelling.)"

Creative firm
Eve Faulkes Design
Morgantown, WV

Client
West Virginia United Methodist Church

Industry
Church

Creative firm
Inertia Graphics
Hagerstown, MD

Client
Potomac Professional Services

Industry
Land Development and Construction Management

Creative firm
Inertia Graphics
Hagerstown, MD

Client
Ledbetter Heights / Rock for Drew

Industry
Music

Creative firm
M3 Advertising Design
Las Vegas, NV

Client
Stone Network

Industry
Industrial, Material Service

MC "It's all here and it's all beautiful. The balance of heavy black to open white space, the graceful curves and the elegant symbolism all combine to give this mark a touch of grace."

RH "A logo that contains, in its vessel shape, a multitude of symbols—and admirably manages to keep them all harmoniously in balance. The execution, with its attention to line weight balance, positive/negative space, and flowing curve construction, is impeccable.

"The one nonsymmetrical element, the eye, is a beautifully considered touch and shows the designer is in full charge of her abilities."

AW "This is a carefully thought out group of symbols. The designer says that the fingers are also dove's wings and flames, both of which represent the Holy Spirit; the fish and cross are also stained glass; the hands are in prayer and a vessel; the pot represents the water turned into wine; and the figure/ground ambiguity represents the relationship of God and man. That's a lot of freight for one little symbol, yet it works admirably."

MC "Drawing from a long history of great rock icons, this mark continues the tradition. The icon is well drawn and powerful, but the insipid type looks like a skinny guy with an insecurity complex."

RH "A technically well-executed logo, with a guitar/angel wing motif that sits happily in a 'rock tradition.' The line of text at the bottom is too light, too letterspaced, and doesn't really need the overly fussy addition of the two dots at either end."

RM "Fantastic illustration. The balance of elements is perfect. The type has a little too much letterspacing, but overall, nice logo."

AW "A mark for a benefit concert features angel wings/long hair/soaring guitars. Excellent craftsmanship."

MC "The mark here is nicely drawn and slightly reminiscent of craftsman era design, which gives it an elegant resonance. The letterspacing in 'WATERSIDE' needs a few tweaks: the 'T-E,' 'R-S,' and 'I-D' pairs need to be tighter to balance the rest."

RH "This looks like a nature reserve instead of a housing development: 'An estate development of multi-million dollar houses, high-end clients. Right off the water and secluded in nature,' which is entirely appropriate when what you're selling is the surrounding natural environment and not just the houses themselves."

RM "The illustration of the foliage almost protecting the leaf is a great concept for this reserve."

MC "The graceful gesture of the calligraphic script here is nicely matched with the serif type. The decay feels a bit artificial, but it works to support the hand-crafted 'designer' feeling of the product."

RH "An evident eye for balance and harmony—note; the angle of the crossbar on the 't' is reflected in the loop below 'NET-WORK'—shows the designer of this logo has a refined eye. As a logo for a stone and marble distribution, business-to-business company, it may have been interesting to execute this logo in real stone and see what a photographic execution would have looked like."

RM "A nice use of type aging helps give this logo and the company it represents heritage."

AW "Lovely lettering and spacing. It all appears to have been equally damaged, so aging treatment was probably done at one time after the shapes had been positioned. The colors seem a bit bright and festive for a distributor of quarried stone and marble: reduce chroma (or intensity) to achieve more stone-like colors."

Creative firm
3
Albuquerque, NM

Client
Rightvue

Industry
Electronics

 Rightvue is a video Web enhancement feature for websites. It connects users with retail websites and vice versa.

RH "This logo evokes the linking of user and client. The two halves link like hooks around each other, and along with an eye, it also manages to contain two arrows pointing left and right."

RM "The use of the connecting eye shapes gives this logo great character and plays off of the company name nicely."

AW "'Eye' plus 'monitor' equals this fine result. The blue space between the white halves is well resolved. I am concerned that it rather strongly evokes the Time Warner eye/ear mark designed by Stefan Geissbuhler in 1990. This similarity would be mitigated if the 'S' in the center—whether in reverse or right reading—stood for something."

Creative firm
Lisa Losken Design Consulting
Green Point, South Africa

Client
Genesys Health

Industry
Holistic Healing

RH "Artificially expanding (stretching) type should be avoided. Here it gives rise to inconsistent stroke widths, specifically the thin strokes on the 'N,' which are now too thick, and the diagonal on the same letter, which is now too thin. Optima is an elegant and refined font which, unlike a more geometric slab sans, is especially unsuited to distortions of this kind. On the plus side, 'health' has been aligned with 'NES'—it would be nice to have enlarged the icon to the same width, too."

RM "A great icon has been made from DNA strands, tying in this icon with the word mark. Color plays a big part in the energy created at the center of the icon."

AW "Fine illustration. Tasty use of color as a connector. However, the letters in 'GENESYS' have been stretched horizontally. There is no 'Optima Expanded' because Hermann Zapf didn't want one—and he reworked the entire font family in 2002 as 'Optima nova,' at which time he did create a condensed version, as well as true italic fonts.

"Stretching type is common because it is so easy to do. But it imposes a significant decrease in letterform elegance: letters are shapes designed by artists who have a heightened feel for proportion. So if you need an expanded face, use one that has been properly designed, not a digitally distorted version of a regular width face."

159

Creative firm
Alambre Estudio
Donostia, Spain

Client
Restaurante Casa Cámara

Industry
Restaurant

 "Bodoni updated by taking out every bit of intercharacter space. Whether or not you like what has been done to these classic letterforms, it is undeniable that it was done on purpose, and intentionality is essential to good design."

Creative firm
Michael Patrick Partners
Palo Alto, CA

Client
Scott Spiker Photography

Industry
Creative Services

 "Very tasteful and very artsy rendition of a creative's mark. The key here are colors chosen, type size contrast, and type style contrast. What makes it work are careful alignments."

Creative firm
A3 Design
Charlotte, NC

Client
DR Horton

Industry
Home Builder

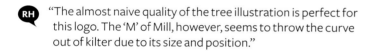
RH "The almost naive quality of the tree illustration is perfect for this logo. The 'M' of Mill, however, seems to throw the curve out of kilter due to its size and position."

RM "The use of distress and aging really gives a sense of longevity. Sometimes, the 'distressed look' can be overdone, but here it is executed perfectly."

AW "Americana expressed as a rubbing from the end of a fruit crate. This is a delightful impression of country living."

Creative firm
Holtz design
Natick, MA

Client
Sally & Fitch LLP

Industry
Law

AW "Interaction, motion, and openness are the messages that come across in this mark for a litigation law firm. The type-face is Trajan, again. It is hard to create a distinctive visual personality if you use the same form as many others. Fortunately, the emphasis here is on the twin curves."

"Fifteen years ago, companies competed on price. Today it's quality.
Tomorrow it's design."

Bob Hayes,
Professor Emeritus,
Harvard Business School

CHAPTER 3
Shelf-Savvy

Retail-Oriented Logos

Creative firm
Brand Engine
Sausalito, CA

Client
SkylarHaley

Industry
Food and Beverage

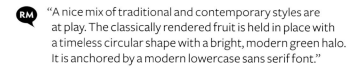
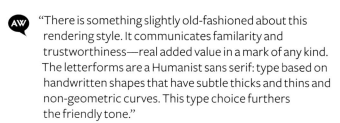

MC "The fruit illustrations used in this series are hyper-real in their juicy perfection. Matching them with the simplistic circle and unadorned lettering gives the series a clean, modern feeling without losing any tastiness. My only critique is a minor one: it looks as if the path around the fruit is slightly off, leaving a white line around some of the fruit."

RH "A realistic portrayal of the fruit, suggesting a natural source for the juice—something a more graphic and therefore, perhaps more artificial portrayal would not communicate."

RM "A nice mix of traditional and contemporary styles are at play. The classically rendered fruit is held in place with a timeless circular shape with a bright, modern green halo. It is anchored by a modern lowercase sans serif font."

AW "There is something slightly old-fashioned about this rendering style. It communicates familiarity and trustworthiness—real added value in a mark of any kind. The letterforms are a Humanist sans serif: type based on handwritten shapes that have subtle thicks and thins and non-geometric curves. This type choice furthers the friendly tone."

Creative firm
Tokyo Farm
Los Angeles, CA

Client
Milk Boutique

Industry
Retail, Fashion

 "The childlike simplicity of this logo is created by a few, quite refined choices, allowing the letters to bleed out of the puddle shape and adding a flower that is just slightly irregular. My only tweak would be increasing the weight of the top stroke of the 'k.' It's a bit thin where it leaves the puddle."

 "Flowing letterforms, fresh colors—this is a playful, summery logo. That it's for a fashion boutique and not milk just adds to the interest. The execution is polished and refined, and the curves and the way they join the type are almost flawlessly executed."

 "Making 'milk' look liquid requires a deft touch where the letters join the perimeter of the pool so neither dominates the other. The inside of the 'm' and the top of the 'k' are nearly right but curve off a bit too quickly, giving the light blue milk priority over the letterforms."

Creative firm
Braue: Strategic Brand Design
Bremerhaven, Germany

Client
Gebrüder Wollenhaupt

Industry
Tea Trading Company

 "Everything is working splendidly here; even the drop shadows are treated with a professional touch. The choice of condensed serif mixed with Copperplate evokes a classic richness perfect for a line of tea. Even the arched type is well handled and spaced. Bravo!"

 "Elegantly balanced execution, great color combination, and a good example of a logo that DOESN'T fall foul of the 'drop shadow more forward in the mix than the letters casting it' rule."

 "Timeless in its classic handling of form and counterform, particularly the generous space between the type's perimeter and the inside of the border."

Creative firm
Korn Design
Boston, MA

Client
Zigo Take Out Food

Industry
Restaurant

 "Oh so close! I like the combination of photographic elements here, but the logo looks like it was stuck on later. If the logo had been printed onto the plate and THEN photographed so there was a little shine and distortion of the letters as they curved up, this logo would go from pretty good to totally great."

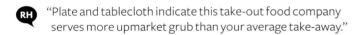 "Plate and tablecloth indicate this take-out food company serves more upmarket grub than your average take-away."

"An actual photo rather than a simplified rendering is a refreshing approach. Note the precise bisection of the plate and 'zigo' by the background: that is a purposeful relationship."

Creative firm
Storm Corporate Design
Auckland, New Zealand

Client
Info Technologies

Industry
IT

 "It's amazing how well this reads considering how much is missing. A software logo is the perfect place to play with geometric abstractions and missing pieces. The designer did a nice job of moving and removing elements to create a feeling of kinetic motion. My only issue is the curve in the 'S'—it needs to be smoothed out just a touch."

 "This logo plays some interesting games with positive and negative space. The 'E' and 'Q' are formed from the same shape, one with the bar dropped. However, there are some areas that, because they've been derived from purely geometric forms, need finessing. For example, the bend in the middle of the 'S' needs smoothing out—getting this part of this letter to look elegant and beautiful is one of the hardest elements of font design."

 "Sequel is an Indian software developer, so the stark on/off feeling of the letterforms is a thoughtful interpretation of a computer's binary language."

Creative firm
zackdesign
Cincinnati, OH

Client
Caraline & Janey Heartfelt Creations

Industry
Home Decor

Creative firm
Crave, Inc.
Boca Raton, FL

Client
Organic Cottage

Industry
Food, Organic Products from India

Creative firm
Crave, Inc.
Boca Raton, FL

Client
Southern Specialties

Industry
Food

Creative firm
Crave, Inc.
Boca Raton, FL

Client
DeLight Bar

Industry
Food

RH "It adds to the handmade quality to have the actual logo made from felt—but look closely and you'll see that the lettering has been added digitally afterward, and is not a part of the photo. This is probably because the letters would be very fiddly to cut out of felt successfully. Getting the perspective correct so the lettering sits flat on the background, would have helped it be more convincing."

AW "A logo crafted to give the truest representation of the business is an obvious direction and gives this mark its charm. The limited color palette helps, too. The super-tight letter spacing in the primary type may be a consequence of the crafting technology, but it disturbs enough to detract from the two unusually spelled names."

MC "This logo looks like organic produce from the American heartland has been given the Bollywood treatment. The type treatment and the containing shapes are completely unrelated.

"The containing shape is quite fun and communicates 'Indian' well, so it isn't necessary to hit the Indian connection too literally with the lettering and symbol, too. Letterforms that were simpler, cleaner, and rounder would work much better here."

AW "The shield shape and coloration is definitely Indian and quite right. But the font choice is skewed to express 'organic' at the expense of adding anything 'Indian' to the mix.

"The leaf drawings should be of Indian origin and agree in style with the type. As a unit, the leaves and type look too small in the shield device."

MC "I love the bright, vibrating orange and pink colors, but I wish the outline around 'PARADISE' was distressed to match the rest of the lettering. As is, it looks like a last-minute legibility fix. The Hawaiian flowers are very cliché—a more unique illustration would have made this logo feel more unique."

AW "Outlined, damaged type is not something you see every day, and it works very well here. In contrast, 'tropicals' doesn't share that treatment, and it looks ordinary.

"The traditional Hawaiian floral motif (I think I have the shirt that was scanned from) might have been replaced with custom-drawn fruits in the same style, since that is the product this company sells. As is, it looks like a fashion company."

MC "The adjusted rough letters are fitted to the swash and leaf ornament in an almost unnoticeable way that really works. But the word 'rawbar' got all the love. The 'deLight' is less delightful; it is too small and randomly placed. No effort was made to make the 'L-i' space work. It feels like an afterthought."

AW "Greatest hit: the way the roughened primary type is bent to agree with the underscore and leaf artwork."

Creative firm
Crave, Inc.
Boca Raton, FL

Client
Southern Selects

Industry
Food, Premium Fresh Produce

 "This is a nice monogram for a produce company and has just the right amount of detail. The ornament suggests leafy greens without resorting to literal lettuce illustrations. However, I wonder if the background orange blend is really necessary?"

 "The best part of this mark is disguised by the light orange and outer green rings. The best part? The way the flourishes highlight the key central stroke of the 'S.' Why is it disguised? Because the negative shapes between the 'S' and the flourishes are thinner than the stroke thickness of the green circles. Thin the circles to match the thinner dimension, and this baby sings!"

Creative firm
Crave, Inc.
Boca Raton, FL

Client
XStream Beverage Group

Industry
Beverage, Energy Drink

 "The illustration suggests, not so subtly, that the main ingredient in this drink might actually work! The type is a nice choice, but I agree that it would be more interesting with a color inline or red/black split. Giving the type a custom treatment would take this from nice typesetting to a great logo."

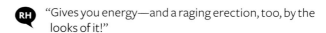 "Gives you energy—and a raging erection, too, by the looks of it!"

 "Given the illustration's style, this is a fine choice of letterforms. But an opportunity has been missed to unify the illustration and type and add to the overall character of the mark. Apply the red/black split of the image into the type—and do something with 'ENERGY DRINK' so it isn't just hanging around down there. Every single element in a logo is an opportunity for the designer to show off how well she or he sees design relationships."

"There's a little too much going on here for easy communication. The attitude is right—big, fat, and shiny—but I wish the shine treatment had been given to the nicely fat and candy-shaped individual letters rather than to the bean shape."

"Though this logo has a logic—it's elastic, and it's made of jelly—the execution could be simpler and therefore bolder. The shine combined with the font (the kitch classic 'Amelia' designed by Stan Davis for VGC in 1967) gives a complex result that could be hard to read. I'd also question the relevance of the random full stops (periods)."

"I love it as is—except for the airplane-window highlights, which fight with the other bright spot highlights near the letterforms' baseline."

Creative firm
Moby Dick Warszawa
Warsaw, Poland

Client
Jutrzenka

Industry
Candy

Bon-ton is a brand created for elastic, jelly candies.

Creative firm
IE Design + Communications
Hermosa Beach, CA

Client
Harmony Organic Frozen Yogurt

Industry
Food

Creative firm
Taylor Design
Stamford, CT

Client
Marble Hill Chocolatier

Industry
Food

Creative firm
Lloyds Graphics Design, Ltd.
Blenheim, New Zealand

Client
Fly Fearless/Lake Chalice

Industry
Winery

Creative firm
Lloyds Graphics Design, Ltd.
Blenheim, New Zealand

Client
Premoli

Industry
Food and Produce

MC "The swash-plus-apple icon is a great idea, but the weights are too thin to relate well with the type. Adding some thick and thin variation to the swash strokes would make it tie in with the weight variations in the logo type. The fonts are nicely chosen, but the subline seems a bit small to work well in most applications."

AW "This composite illustration puts an apple on top of a cone-shaped calligraphic flourish for a one-off abstracted fro-yo mark. The font used in the primary type suggests a youthful target market, but the secondary type is mystifying in its font choice and size. The only thing that works there is the color, which relates it to the artwork."

MC "The bounced 'B' is a surprising touch that adds a bit of humor to an otherwise rather stately type treatment and makes the slightly cartoonish printer's dingbat work. The letter-spacing needs a few tweaks though. The space around the 'A' in 'Marble' is a bit too wide, and the bounced-up 'B' is a bit too tight."

AW "This is a chocolate lounge in Ohio, so its echos of Starbucks—especially in use of color—are grounded in sense. The hiccuping 'B' is enough of a defining focal point that it fights with the printer's flower. It would work better if the flower were larger—as wide as 'CHOCOLATIER.'"

MC "I like the casual approach to this wine logo. The black bird and white type work well against the 'chipboard' brown background. I like the tension created by the edginess of a black bird countered by the word 'fearless' in white. The irregular 'typewriter' tagline gives the label an authentic, no-frills feeling. I'd expect the wine to be a bit unusual, but good."

AW "This mark is noteworthy because it doesn't look like a wine brand. It is getting increasingly difficult to differentiate a wine product, in part because of just these kinds of nontraditional approaches. This one cuts through the competing voices."

MC "Nice choice of colors for olive oil products—the green gold is just right. The choice of type suggests Old World but retains a modern feeling. I could get nitpicky about the letterspacing between the 'P' and 'r,' but it seems unnecessary given how well everything else is working here."

RM "This logo appears to have three colors but could consolidate to two since there are two dark green values that are fairly close. The letterspacing between the 'P' and the 'r' in 'Premoli' could be tightened; otherwise, it's a nice execution. I like the friendly curl on the letterforms and the 'o' even has an olive pimento."

AW "Nice shapes throughout. But what defines the excellence of this mark is the management of negative space, which is very well handled."

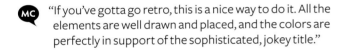

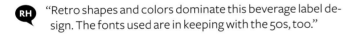

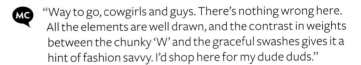

Creative firm
Fauxkoi Design Company
Minneapolis, MN

Client
Anodyne

Industry
Beverage

MC — "If you've gotta go retro, this is a nice way to do it. All the elements are well drawn and placed, and the colors are perfectly in support of the sophisticated, jokey title."

RH — "Retro shapes and colors dominate this beverage label design. The fonts used are in keeping with the 50s, too."

AW — "Anodyne is a humorous name for a beverage company. It means 'a pain-killing drug' and also 'not likely to provoke offense.' This logo is an ideal expression of the latter: every part is well visualized, formulated, and placed. Okay, the 'mpls' and 'minn' could be a little lower to agree with the linespacing between 'ANODYNE' and 'BEVERAGE.'"

Creative firm
Fauxkoi Design Company
Minneapolis, MN

Client
Andrew Grant

Industry
Retail

MC — "Way to go, cowgirls and guys. There's nothing wrong here. All the elements are well drawn, and the contrast in weights between the chunky 'W' and the graceful swashes gives it a hint of fashion savvy. I'd shop here for my dude duds."

RH — "An elegantly executed simple monogram using a traditional 'western' flavored font with sheriff badge stars."

AW — "Appropriate charm for a small retail store specializing in southwestern goods. Greatest hit: the off-center star."

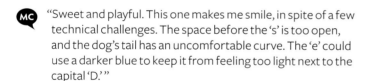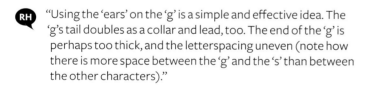

Creative firm
Yiying Design
New South Wales, Australia

Client
edog online shop

Industry
Retail

MC "Sweet and playful. This one makes me smile, in spite of a few technical challenges. The space before the 's' is too open, and the dog's tail has an uncomfortable curve. The 'e' could use a darker blue to keep it from feeling too light next to the capital 'D.'"

RH "Using the 'ears' on the 'g' is a simple and effective idea. The 'g's tail doubles as a collar and lead, too. The end of the 'g' is perhaps too thick, and the letterspacing uneven (note how there is more space between the 'g' and the 's' than between the other characters)."

RM "This logo is not perfectly executed, but it has the right intent. The relationship of the dog's nose, eyes, and ears are well placed within the circle of the 'g' and carry enough information to get the job done."

AW "Delightful. Pull one ear up a bit to tuck the 's' in. And reclaim the original bottom half of the 'g,' which has been thickened here for some reason."

Creative firm
Tiago Teixeira Design
Oporto, Portugal

Client
Perto do Rio

Industry
Fashion

MC "There are several very sophisticated ingredients on this hang tag. The graceful symbol uses abstract asymmetry to make a strong statement that is balanced by the high-tech type choice. The thin weight of the type supports the high-end feeling and the random thread adds a touch of the unexpected. All of these elements are balanced by the huge areas of black space that give the layout a feeling of restrained but elegant minimalism."

RH "The random thread adds an interesting touch to this fashion logo—though it might be too fine to reproduce at a small size. Keep those swing tickets large."

Creative firm
Brand Engine
Sausalito, CA

Client
Frontier Natural Foods

Industry
Food

 "The lettering here is very elegantly done. The weights of the capitals are well balanced to the lowercase, and the missing dot and slices keep it from feeling too heavy in any one spot."

"The choice of lowercase serif adds a warmth and friendliness to support the fresh organic feeling of the botanical art."

 "Again, the use of a fine hand-executed illustration emphasizes the organic and the natural. The type is elegantly combined, using the tail of the 'y' as the i-dot and interlinking the 'O' and the 'S' into a monogram."

 "The illustration appears as though it was pulled from a classic botanical book. The interlocking letterforms do not hinder overall readability and their positioning creates a well-anchored pyramid shape that refuses to budge."

 "A wonderfully drawn illustration with equally thoughtful type makes this a terrific mark. The 'missing' slices of the 'S' and 'O' are wider than we might normally expect—then it becomes evident they are echoing the letterspacing and helping lighten the color of the ligature so it doesn't overwhelm the rest of the type area. I would slide the 'l' over a touch to the left to equalize its spacing between the 'p' and the 'y.'"

Creative firm
Brand Engine
Sausalito, CA

Client
Tribeca Kitchens

Industry
Food

 "The 'Plum' script is well drawn and has a nice, graceful gesture to it. The little leaf adds the perfect, memorable touch. However, the word 'organics' got the orphan child treatment. It's too light, and the style doesn't relate well. It looks like the font defaulted."

 "The 'Plum' is great—the green ear a delightful suprise. But aside from its unifying color, what is right about 'organics'? It could be a little bigger or a little smaller, a little more letterspaced or a little less, a little bolder or a little lighter. In short, with so many 'six of ones or a half dozen of the others,' it isn't resolved."

Creative firm
Brand Engine
Sausalito, CA

Client
PMO Wildwood

Industry
Food

 "What is it with the drop shadows? This is a very nicely executed logo and would be quite readable without the shadow. Sometimes good design is knowing when to stop."

 "It's a little slick for an organic outfit, but its swashes and customization are handsomely worked."

Creative firm
Brand Engine
Sausalito, CA

Client
Pixie Maté

Industry
Food

 "This is a well-crafted mark that evokes the retro style of the 40s to communicate a sense of fun. The bright colors will be great at getting attention."

 "Maté is a caffeinated infusion prepared by steeping dried leaves of erva-maté (Portuguese) and yerba maté (Spanish) (*Ilex paraguariensis*) in hot water. (I pinched that from Wikipedia.)

"In contrast to the previous tea logos that emphasised their natural sources, this logo takes a bold and punchy approach, probably to emphasise the caffeine kick. The stars resemble the visual effects Herge uses in the Tintin comics when a character gets hit over the head or is groggy and dizzy—all effects that caffeine have on me."

 "I always look first at the smallest detail to see whether a design has been thoughtfully finished. In this case, 'the smallest detail' is the way the stars relate to the golden circle. Both are carefully, symmetrically placed, so it is likely the other relationships of both form and counterform are as well crafted. And they are."

Creative firm
Brand Engine
Sausalito, CA

Client
Mighty Leaf Tea Company

Industry
Bath and Spa Products

 "This logo has a nice flow and gesture to it. The repeated forms contribute to its unity. I'm not sure tea for bathing should look quite this rough, but that's just me."

 "Rough type = natural ingredients. The repeated 'a' gives the game away that this is not in fact hand drawn, but a font. The texture has been consistently taken across to the other elements of the logo, though again, close examination reveals that the swoosh underline is flipped and repeated."

 "The leaf serves as the dot over the 'i,' unifying art and type. The muted mint green is a calming color choice."

Creative firm
Turner Duckworth
London, UK

Client
BOA Housewares

Industry
Housewares

 "This is a simple and clever approach—it suggests what the product does without wasting words or decoration. The letterforms are simple, but unique enough to create differentiation and ownership."

 "A nice example of using the product as the logo or, in this case, the product's target—a ring pull on a can.

"The shape of the 'c' is echoed in the 'a' and 'p,' giving the custom type an internal cohesion. The 'u' has been narrowed effectively to retain a good negative/positive internal/external balance.

"There are, however, letterspacing issues—the 'c' and the 'a' are further apart by necessity of incorporating the circle, which could have been resolved by possibly using a wider spacing on the 'anpull.' This wider spacing may have said 'elegance' instead of 'practicality,' however. Balancing these messages successfully is something designers have to consider carefully."

 "This is a clever identity that delivers on a very simple name and idea. I appreciate the visual representation of the product and the carefully selected (and altered) letterforms."

 "Distinctive type based on the shape of the hole makes this a worthy mark. Using a suitably 'invisible' secondary face for additional copy is essential to avoid typographic competition."

181

NATURALLY
ACTIVE
MEN'S SKINCARE

Creative firm
Fargo Design Co., Inc.
McKees Rocks, PA

Client
Jackson Hole Trading Co.

Industry
Home Decor

Creative firm
Turner Duckworth
London, UK

Client
Liz Earle Cosmetics Ltd.

Industry
Skincare

Creative firm
Brand Engine
Sausalito, CA

Client
Karma Creations

Industry
Retail, Home Accessories Store

Creative firm
IE Design + Communications
Hermosa Beach, CA

Client
Theresa Kathryn

Industry
Fashion

 "I love the hand-drawn lettering used here. It's perfectly funky and gives a nicely contemporary twist to the age-old cowboy metaphor. I wish the horseshoe and ornaments were hand drawn to match. The colors are nicely chosen as well."

 "Jackson Hole is owned and operated by environmental enthusiasts and practices 'earth-friendly' processes. This is reflected in the earthy, handmade quality of the type.

"If you look at the two 'O's, you'll see that they're actually not hand drawn, but a font—and the clip art horseshoe and flourishes, which depart from the hand-drawn aesthetic, also detract from the consistent execution of the idea.

"The colors are suitably natural. There are some spacing issues with the stars on the tagline."

 "The essence of the attitude and experience of Jackson Hole, a premiere destination, must be communicated in this mark. It kind of looks like a sketch for the finished logo, because the 'clean' art and swashes are mismatched with the pseudo-rough letterforms. Let's do this right: have a piece of leather hand-tooled, then photograph it."

NATURALLY
ACTIVE
MEN'S SKINCARE

 "This company's location is in the Isle of Wight (which helped inspire the logo, a leaf transforming into the crest of a wave). Unfortunately, the wave is much more obvious than the leaf, and the ball serif on the leaf twig also suggests a 'C' monogram, further confusing the issue. A consistent type style, using a change of point size only for emphasis, adds elegance."

 "The 'C' shape is unavoidable, though this is a finely crafted mark. The choice of typeface is not immediately discernible—something with more roundness at the terminals would relate it better to the wave/leaf top, which is where the focus is."

 "There is a strong, dynamic energy to the brushstroke initials in this mark. They contrast nicely with the clean type, but the lightweight 'Kathryn' with the capital 'K' throws off the weights and heights. It feels like one thing too many going on when the focus should be on the initials. Either a lowercase 'k' or an all caps treatment throughout would have been a more comfortable solution."

 "Purposeful design contrasts used throughout: spontaneous brushstrokes vs. geometric sans serif letterforms, bold vs. light, caps vs. lowercase. But the contrasts are balanced with similarities: shared overall width, common all-black color, matched cap height and x-height. The only dissonant note is the cap 'K' where a lowercase 'k' should be in 'Kathryn.'"

 "The swashed letterforms in this logo are very gracefully placed, but there are some weight issues that might keep it from reaching nirvana. The diagonal strokes of the 'M' are too heavy for the rest of the letters, and the curved top of the 'A' is too thin. The lower 'K' into 'M' also needs a bit of attention to the positioning of the thin area."

 "A fine serif with calligraphic additions. The curves flow throughout the logo, even when broken. For example, from the 'M' to the apex of the 'A.' The swashes become just a wee bit too fine at the base of the 'R' and the end of the swash on the top of the 'A' in relation to the serifs."

 "Karma, from the Sanskrit for 'effect' or 'fate,' is a core tenet of Hinduism and Buddhism. It says that the sum of a person's actions in this and previous lives decides his or her fate in future existences. So a mark that curves back on itself, as this one does, is perfectly illustrative."

Creative firm
Turner Duckworth
London, UK

Client
Waitrose

Industry
Pets

MC "I'm not sure my cat would think this was funny, but he might be the only one! This is a nicely executed and amusing approach. The slight dent in the metal and the off-rotated screw heads add details that expand the humor."

RH "A cat litter logo that extends the familiar toilet door symbols to our favorite pets. A strong concept well executed, and one of the few instances where a photoshop textured and shaded effect is entirely appropriate."

RM "Although I'm not a fan of logos that are rendered using multiple photoshop filters, I can't help but think that this bold, iconic cat shape wouldn't necessarily translate well in any other way. A clever concept."

AW "Delightful idea and execution. A well-loved cat wears a collar and tag: pity this tag, which is nearly the exact size of the two screws but doesn't align with them. That subtle lack is not a bad level of weakness!"

Creative firm
Crave, Inc
Boca Raton, FL

Client
Vuru

Industry
Vitamins and Supplements

 "I feel happy and healthy looking at this mark. The vitamin flower is a very cheerful way to take a pill, and the type goes along with the upbeat mood very nicely."

 "Beautiful sunny choice of colors, and the inclusion of a fresh lime green really makes the palette sing. Life and vitality."

 "The designer has created a logo that communicates well on a number of levels. The color palette uses bright hues and tones synonymous with nature. The pills have been arranged in perfect balance and create a simplified flower or sun shape. Regardless of which shape you see, the visual is inherently appropriate."

 "This mark for a vitamin brand uses pills as a flower or as a sun, either of which is a potent symbol of health and vitality. The rounded ends of the letterforms relate to the oval pill shapes."

Creative firm
DOHM
Kew, UK

Client
Ransom

Industry
Healthcare

 "The 'M' here has been shaped to resemble both a baby's bottom and a heart, representing loving care. The letter-shapes resemble squeezed ointment from a tube, and the rounded curves of the font (VAG Rounded) are suitably soft and baby-friendly."

 "The designer's statement says, 'Metanium Ointment soothes and treats your baby's nappy rash.' I don't know what a 'nappy rash' is, but the electric blueness of this dimensional type sure suggests cleanliness and medical certainty."

Creative firm
DOHM
Kew, UK

Client
Lifes2good

Industry
Packaging

Creative firm
Siquis
Baltimore, MD

Client
Earth Shoes

Industry
Footwear

Creative firm
Siquis
Baltimore, MD

Client
Greg Bennett

Industry
Footwear

Creative firm
OCTODESIGN
Jakarta, Indonesia

Client
Bali Island

Industry
Province (Destination Branding)

RH "Nourella is a skin nutrition program to rejuvenate and maintain youthful skin 'from outside in.' This is represented by a face that also doubles as a clock face, indicating turning back the clock on the aging process. A subtle skin-colored grad and lilac Optima type lend a suitably feminine and refined cosmetic appearance."

AW "Nice alignment of the face's forehead up through the vertical stroke of the 'T.' But this is mitigated by the mismatched type size and spaciousness in the two halves of the clock's indices."

MC "This logo has a good, earth-friendly feeling created by the color choice as well as the elements. I wish the fish and elephant were less 'streamlined/autotraced' and matched a bit better with the more authentic, hand-drawn texture of the font. The lack of distressed texture inside the animals, earth, and globe makes them feel more computer-y and less truly distressed."

RH "...And another of my fonts! This time it's Mulgrave. Mulgrave has a gritty texture that has been taken here across to the other elements; this effect would have been more successful if the grit had retained the same degree of detail throughout."

AW "Wonderful that this is crooked. It says, 'Earth is in the balance.' It would be nice if the flecks of crud that came with each of the three components—dust with the type, sand with the animals, and pebbles with the globe, were all scaled equally to disguise their separate provenances.

"Design is not simply a matter of adding precooked ingredients: we need to make them work together seamlessly. Or, as American composer Aaron Copland said, 'The point of composition is to make the result seem inevitable.' "

RH "I'm playing 'spot my font' and here we have Chase again. I'll be checking the royalty statements! The counters (internal 'holes' in type) have here been dropped out, presumably to emphasize the vernacular quality of the design, and arrows have been added to indicate trail directions. The smaller arrows would benefit from being larger and more logically aligned with the type."

AW "I agree that the three small arrows should be the same size as the north arrow. But I think the off-kilter placement of these three contributes to the feeling of being lost and needing direction. It may, in fact, be the most distinctive attribute of this mark."

MC "There's lots to love about the shape and ornament in this logo. Balancing lettering inside such an ornate symmetrical shape is a design challenge that succeeds at first glance but falls down slightly when you look at the details.

"It looks as if the red ornament was a found design, left untouched by the designer, while the lettering was forced to conform to it. The result is an off-center feeling to the 'L,' irregular widths on the white comstock around the letters and some awkward curly ends on the lettering that don't quite match the ornament. Adjusting both elements to work together could have corrected some of these uncomfortable details."

RH "A well-thought-through rationale underpins this logo. Generally, it's also beautufully executed, though the necessarily off-center 'L' is somewhat inelegant, and the 'B's overt resemblance to a '3' could confuse. The tagline is somewhat weedy in appearance."

AW "Everything about this mark has been considered. According to the designer's statement, the triangle shape references the three Gods of the universe and the three casts of nature. The lettering uses Balinese traditional written forms. The colors are chosen to represent the Brahma God, the Wisnu God and the Siwa God. 'SHANTI SHANTI SHANTI' is derived from a Hindu prayer that, when said three times, is believed to bring peace and harmony.

"The symmetry of the 'B' and the highly stylized 'i' are fine touches. The three words across the bottom look too spindly and thin."

187

Creative firm
Kinesis, Inc.
Ashland, OR

Client
Sweetgrass Natural Fibers

Industry
Clothing Company

 "The simplicity of this design is also its strength. The choice of typeface with its tall 't' and straight 'w' matches nicely with the blades of grass, and the sophisticated colors keep it from being overly sweet."

 "Stroke equivalency between the illustration and primary type, and conscientious spacing in the secondary type to jump over the loop of the 'g' make this a well-crafted mark."

Creative firm
Firebelly Design
Chicago, IL

Client
Awakening Organics

Industry
Apparel

 "The curved strokes and super-thin weights in this lettering, combined with the friendly, open round shapes of both 'a's, the 'e', and the 'g' make it feel inviting and healthy. The italic gives it a sense of forward movement and optimism—perfect for organic clothing for kids."

 "Elegantly executed. The leaf icon doesn't impede reading the logo as a whole at all. The letter curves are beautifully smooth and flowing."

 "A nice mark. Nothing random about it and plenty added to make it distinctive."

Creative firm .
Paragon Marketing Communications
Salmiya, Kuwait

Client
LaBaguette

Industry
Bakery

 "Dual-language logos pose a unique set of problems.
Getting a good combination involves a careful balance of
line weights and letter shapes. Here, close attention to this
issue has resulted in a beautifully elegant result."

 "This mark for a chain of bakeries in Kuwait is handsomely
resolved. 'Since 1983' looks misplaced, and that it appears to
be the same width as the artwork begs for it to be centered.
Pity there's a descender in the way."

Creative firm
Lucidamedia, Ltd.
London, UK

Client
Fresh

Industry
Salon Products

 "This logo leaves out just enough to catch your eye and
make you look again. The designer resisted the impulse to
add leaves or other obvious symbols and instead opted
for sophisticated abstraction. Choosing a font with subtle
weight variation gives it an elegance that a mono-weight
font wouldn't have."

 "A lovely example of leaving out parts that become the
focal point. The letterspacing of both the primary and
the secondary type is used as a relating attribute."

Creative firm
face
Harrogate, UK

Client
Snugpak

Industry
Sleeping Bag Manufacturer

Creative firm
Shine Advertising Company
Madison, WI

Client
Visions Windows & Doors

Industry
Window Manufacturing

QUA
BATHS & SPA

Creative firm
Addis Creson
Berkeley, CA

Client
Harrah's

Industry
Health Spa

Creative firm
Shine Advertising Company
Madison, WI

Client
Auburn Ridge

Industry
Cabinetry

MC "This mark is simple and bold. The snail is a great symbol for the comfort and security suggested by the name. The bold line weights will allow it to be applied as an embroidered patch, as well as silk-screened easily—important considerations for an outdoor equipment and apparel business."

RH "A snail shell, the ultimate portable home, is a fitting logo for snug sleeping bags, rucksacks, and outdoor clothing. The spiral here is drawn in Adobe Illustrator using the Spiral tool. Rather than a true spiral, however, it is actually made from a series of joined quarter circles, which unfortunately, gives it a slightly lumpy appearance."

QUA

MC "This logo has a wonderful, soft, watercolor feeling that suggests pools of water or a piece of modern art. Before reading the designer's description about the three Roman baths, it reminded me of a pile of pebbles, like a cairn along a trail that marks the way, which is also an appropriate symbol for 'qua' or 'here.'

"The subtle use of different blues for the three spots gives this mark an added appeal, and the slight unbalanced feeling of the stack of three gives it movement. Very nice!"

RH "The designer of this logo writes: '*Qua* means "here" in Italian and is also evocative of "aqua," or water. The name captures the importance of all members of Roman society meeting at the baths. Building upon the vision of the brand we created a meaningful identity that symbolically reinforced the three pools of the Roman baths.'

"I showed this around the studio, and no one saw it as representative of three Roman baths. This is a good example of a rationale sounding solid but failing the 'man (or woman) in the street' test. If the rationale still gives rise to an intriguing and memorable logo that can stand on its own visual merits, though, all is forgiven. With its natural shapes resembling blobs of watercolor paint, this one makes the grade."

AW "Having an idea for a design is always better than merely decorating or making a random solution. That the idea for this mark is obscured still leaves an inspired mark, largely because of the styling of the three pools of water."

MC "There's an odd lack of consistency to this lettering, in addition to a seeming lack of concept to the logo overall. The tops of the 'i's are rounded, while the ends of the strokes of all the other letters are flat. Why not add this subtlety to the rest of the letters or leave it out consistently?

"The 's's feel a bit too heavy for the rest of the letters as well—a result of the complexity of the shape; a simple 's' would have blended better with the rest of the letters."

RH "A design without a strong concept that is, however, beautifully constructed."

AW "This combination of sans serifs works because the primary type is a decorative face—that is, it has sufficient peculiarities to exclude its use at text sizes or for lengthy passages at any size."

MC "This logo is nicely designed and well spaced but lacks a certain originality and flair. It looks like a mark that would work well stamped on the bottom of fine cabinetry, but it suggests that the design of the cabinetry itself might be a bit uninspired."

RH "A nicely executed woodcut illustration is the centerpiece of this Victorian pastiche."

AW "Here's a mark in which there is nothing whatsoever wrong. It is rather handsome, but it lacks a certain distinction, showing the need for a quirk or unique kink in the execution of any logo to separate that one mark from similar designs."

Creative firm
Pearlfisher
London, UK

Client
Nude

Industry
Cosmetics, Health and Beauty

Creative firm
Dustin Commer
Wichita, KS

Client
BH Innovations

Industry
Wood Products

Creative firm
Dustin Commer
Wichita, KS

Client
Har-Son Technologies

Industry
Protective Clothing

Creative firm
Dustin Commer
Wichita, KS

Client
Tape Mouse

Industry
Construction

MC "There's absolutely nothing here that isn't needed, and what's left is elegantly considered. The color, the minimalism, and the rounded forms all work together to support the idea behind the word.

"This mark has the timelessness and simplicity of the Chanel 'C's and the Fendi 'F's. It's a wonderful example of exploiting resonances of shape and using arrangement to create iconic strength. I hope the products are as good as the mark."

RH "A nude color scheme is the finishing touch to this elegantly designed logo. The letters are spelled out using one shape in each of its possible 90-degree rotations. The repetition of the word 'nude' doubles as the crossbar on the 'E' and guarantees no one can misread it."

AW "Very nice. With a little effort, I can imagine a highly abstracted, even cubist, human figure in these shapes… pity it isn't intentionally caused by the design itself."

RH "The buzz saw is such a strong shape that it has achieved a classic status in icon design. Here we have two arrows to further indicate rotation. The type would look better if it had been distorted to fit the circle rather than merely run along a circular baseline, and the inconsistent and pale outline on 'SAW 'N' (more correctly 'N') is an unnecessary addition."

AW "Fine illustration and really fine color combination. Though the typeface is a good choice because it is inspired by handpainted signs from the 1940s, the type is placed in an insensitive way. And the 'Z' in the middle could easily have been rotated to become the apostrophed 'N' in the name, thereby building leterforms into the illustration."

MC "This tape mouse has attitude! It's a great illustration that evokes both aggression and fun at the same time through line style and color choice.

"The tape-measure nose is a really nice touch, and the use of a consistent blue outline for both the illustration and the type makes the whole thing hang together well."

RH "A lively, unpretentious, and practical-looking logo for a lively, unpretentious, and practical product. An effective use of two colors, as well. The line widths are nicely balanced and show careful variation. One small criticism would be the 'dropshadow more forward in the mix than the letters casting it' issue again."

RH "The rhino looks suitably mean and tough, and the peel-off motif indicates a removable skin, but what makes this logo appealing is the tagline—it says exactly what the product does and manages it with humor. The colors look simple and practical. The red drop shadow on the type is the only element that looks poorly executed and out of place—drop the drop shadow, and this logo would be even punchier."

AW "The convincingly drawn peel-off label makes this mark special. Rynoskin is, according to the designer's statement, a manufacturer of 'protective undergarments.' That is certainly a niche market I never considered."

AW "This product, a tape measure that can 'mouse over' materials and not get stuck, deserves exactly this kind of dynamic, lighthearted treatment. There's a little problem with the third stroke of the 'm,' however. I think it is supposed to look like it is behind the tape, but its end runs parallel to the edge of the tape for an awkward relationship."

Creative firm
Watts Design
South Melbourne, Australia

Client
Whole Kids

Industry
Kids Organic Health Foods

 "A very good example of how to successfully design a bold, simple, punchy logo with balance and attention to detail. The varying line weights are balanced overall, there are no areas that are relatively too detailed or too simple, and the colors are unfussy but beautiful. The only less-than-successful element is the tagline, which could be thicker and bolder."

 "Very nice work. The primary type was drawn in Illustrator and deserves a little finessing on the 'e,' 'd,' and especially the 's,' which have crunchy curves that should be smoothed out."

Creative firm
Watts Design
South Melbourne, Australia

Client
Goodman Skincare

Industry
Skincare

 "The customization of the type in this logo should have been done with a bit more sensitivity. The adjustment to the bottom of the 'g' is too heavy for the rest of the font and blends awkwardly from thick to thin. The icon seems a bit foreign to the type as well. Possibly adding some weight variation to the stamens would tie it in a bit better."

 "Typesetting is fine for headlines in magazines, but logos deserve so much more customization. This mark adds swashes and an adjusted letterform shape to Zuzana Licko's 'Mrs. Eaves' typeface with great sensitivity."

Creative firm
Glitschka Studios
Salem, OR

Client
Schier Products

Industry
Plumbing Wholesaler

RH "The simple type here is a perfect counterpoint to the beautiful, woodcut-inspired illustration. Plumbers are practical rugged types, we presume, and this logo looks practical and rugged."

RM "This appears to be a Michael Schwab–inspired logo that even uses a similar vertical poster shape that has become his signature. That being said, I give points to the illustrator's rendering, which is well executed, and I feel that, overall, the logo has good balance."

AW "If we weren't told this was a mark for a plumbing wholesaler, I wouldn't have guessed it. That doesn't mean plumbing marks always have to have pipes and wrenches, but because this isn't a multinational conglomerate, a little hint at its specialty is appropriate.

"Otherwise, the mark could be perceived as a random solution. There is a little too much blackness at the bottom of this otherwise tasty mark."

Creative firm
Glitschka Studios
Salem, OR

Client
Romer Beverage Company

Industry
Food and Beverage

RH "This is a beautiful and elegant example of what might be called a 'heritage' logo. The line weights relate to the type. The negative space is balanced—note how the three lines under the central ribbon serve as a shadow but also to close up what would otherwise be empty space. The finer detailing adds texture without undue complexity. That's attention to detail.

"My only criticism, and it's a very minor one, is the overlarge lower serif on the 'E.' Might it have been possible to reduce it and so center the 'M'?"

RM "All of the elements are present to pull off this classic-shaped logo. It's only missing two facing griffins. Great color selection and overall visual balance. The gray floral pattern behind the crown seems a bit too congested and could probably be simplified a bit."

AW "Excellent use of two colors: every combination has been used, and that brings vitality and depth."

Creative firm
Donatelli + Associates
Hillsboro, OR

Client
Hoyt Arboretum

Industry
Arboretum

Creative firm
Donatelli + Associates
Hillsboro, OR

Client
Hoyt Arboretum

Industry
Arboretum

 MC " 'A world of trees for all seasons' is perfectly expressed in the circle of flowing leaves. The two-color treatment gives the leaves movement and a feeling of depth. The type is also a nice choice; the serifs give the logo a feeling of academic authority, but the lowercase keeps it friendly. The space between the 'y' and 't' in 'Hoyt' and the 'A' and 'r' in 'Arboretum' could be tighter to balance the rest of the spacing, but otherwise, this is a very nicely executed logo."

RH "A circle of playful and beautifully executed leaves encloses a shady space, inviting us to experience this arboretum. The type and spacing are also carefully considered, and the simple, two-color scheme is all that is necessary."

AW "Magnificent illustration, including the negative space. This handsome typeface is ITC Berkeley Oldstyle, Tony Stan's revival of Frederick Goudy's 1938 typeface made for the University of California. I wouldn't mind if the secondary type were closer and as wide as 'Arboretum.'"

RH "Geometric leaves, simply laid out, provide an effective background. The '75' produces a few inelegant small shapes as it crops and overlays this background, but these have been carefully considered and minimized."

AW "The best part of this is the active use of negative space."

Creative firm
Blacktop Creative
Kansas City, MO

Client
H&R Block

Industry
Finance, Tax Preparation

 "A bold and simple execution—very powerful. The gray '50' is somewhat limp; however, using two colors instead of three would simplify it further. I'd like to see this with a green '50' and a black (or navy blue) top square. Setting 'BLOCK' in the same condensed font as '50' would finesse it even further."

 "Consistent width unites these three unrelated components into a single vertical mark. The black figures in front of the gray '50' come forward because of 'atmospheric perspective,' a treatment in which distant objects appear muted and with less contrast because of crudlets in the air."

Creative firm
Glitschka Studios
Salem, OR

Client
QuickSilver Clothing

Industry
Community Outreach

 "Type that manages to look handmade and simply executed but still works is hard to pull off. Though it appears childish, this type is obviously the work of a designer who knows his balance and harmony.

"The interlinked figures show both community and the sharing of ideas. The colors are simple and effective. Would it have been even better to render 'PROJECT' in a hand-drawn style, too? It's the only element that isn't."

 "QuickSilver Clothing developed an outreach program called 'Komunity Project.' So the client liked the misspelling with the 'K,' and the designer persuaded them to drop one of the 'm's. Probably very appropriate for the target audience, given QuickSilver's product line.

"PS: fabulous illustration treatment."

Creative firm
Blacktop Creative
Kansas City, MO

Client
Coca-Cola

Industry
Beverage

 "There's a very nice balance of bold black-and-white space here that makes additional colors completely unnecessary. The texture adds a nice retro touch that works well with the industrial font choices and 'bolts' that seem to hold the logo in place."

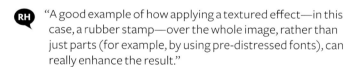 "A good example of how applying a textured effect—in this case, a rubber stamp—over the whole image, rather than just parts (for example, by using pre-distressed fonts), can really enhance the result."

AW "There is no mention of the sponsor, the Coca-Cola Company, so we have to look at this purely on its own merits.

"Interrupting 'BRIDGE' this way is tricky and succeeds because the letterparts necessary for legibility have been preserved in a more or less natural-looking way. This looks like a print was actually repeatedly duplicated on a copy machine in order to accumulate residual damage caused by the copying process itself."

Creative firm
Blacktop Creative
Kansas City, MO

Client
Corbin Bronze

Industry
Sculpture, Furniture, Lighting

MC "The contrast between the doodled, Giacometti-like figure and the super-clean type makes for a nice tension, but the placement of the elements makes me uncomfortable. Why create an almost-centered layout and then mess it up with the 'LTD'? This awkwardness seems to suggest that a more asymmetrical layout might have worked better."

RH "Sometimes ITC Avant Garde, an iconic typeface that cannot be separated from the early 1970s when it was introduced, has its uses. This handsome contrast between austere geometry and organic impressionism looks quite intentional."

AW "An intriguing image—a rough doodle of a figure presumably referencing Tom Corbin's sculptures, furniture, and lighting—is let down by lackluster type. The LTD is given undue prominence by being in color. Would more interesting results not have been achieved if the designer had executed the type in a similar fashion to the image?"

Creative firm
Storm Corporate Design
Auckland, New Zealand

Client
Food For Less Supermarket

Industry
Supermarket

RH "Any bargain-basement product or company runs the risk of thinking they need a bargain-basement logo. This excellent design proves it's possible to say 'cheap and cheerful' without descending into ugliness. The simple layout and the use of empty space above allow a straightforward execution to breathe. Cheap, but not tacky."

AW "I love the sharp black rectangle breaking out of—or into— the rounded red square. Herb Lubalin's Avant Garde typeface, used in 'FOR LESS,' was chosen presumably because it shares the geometricity—partly disguised by missing pieces—in 'FOOD.' Aside from their geometric perfection, they aren't enough alike."

Creative firm
Ian Lynam Design
Tokyo, Japan

Client
Coldplay/Signatures Network

Industry
Music

Creative firm
The Decoder Ring
Austin, TX

Client
What's your vine? Clothing

Industry
Retail, Apparel

 "This band has a lot invested in its branding, so a variation on its theme is appropriate. I wonder whether Coldplay's fans are familiar with making 'grunge' fonts, the massive type design wave in the 1990s brought on by the Macintosh. If so, they'll know what they're looking at. If not, it's a pleasant decoration."

 "Simple idea, nicely executed."

 "The leaves have slightly odd thicks and thins that should as fluidly and effortlessly swell as the magnificent question mark."

Creative firm
Helena Seo Design
Sunnyvale, CA

Client
The Branding Farm / Kind Group

Industry
Fashion

MC "I hope the blue fade is part of the label and hangtag. Without it, this logo loses its best reason for being. Legibility is a bit of an issue too, but I like that the regularity of the letterforms suggests waves or ripples without being too literal."

RH "Another logo that needs to be adjusted to pass the 'man in the street' readability test. SUNEO? SAVO?"

AW "Wavelike forms and whitecap rough edges define this mark for an upscale women's beachwear designer. I cannot tell whether the fading blue box is a required shape or just a convenience in this showing. The mark is far more dynamic by cropping off the top or bottom third of the square."

Creative firm
Shell Graphix
Gold Coast, Queensland, Australia

Client
Learning Seed

Industry
Entertainment

RH "Stretched or squashed type is generally not a good idea—type designers design pre-condensed and pre-extended fonts where the stroke widths and general balance of the design have been finely adjusted. Here, Futura has been stretched to fit the second line, awkwardly contrasting with the non-stretched Futura above."

AW "Excellent formal contrast between geometric letterforms and a wispy, organic leaf."

Creative firm
DOHM
Kew, UK

Client
Barking Mad & Co.

Industry
Gardening

Creative firm
10 Associates, Ltd.
Huddersfield, UK

Client
Black Cat Fireworks, Ltd.

Industry
Fireworks

Creative firm
nealedesign
Wellington, NZ

Client
Miramar Fruit Supplier

Industry
Food

Creative firm
Donatelli + Associates
Hillsboro, OR

Client
Zeba Chocolates

Industry
Food

RH "Barking Mad—a company that supplies bark for gardens. A clever name that needs a suitably lighthearted logo. Here we have a literal interpretation of a mad dog—the madness indicated by crossed eyes and a Tintin-esque squiggle and star above his head."

AW "A pun for a name is a bit misdirected to begin with. That the true nature of the product or company isn't revealed in its mark adds additional confusion. So this mark, for a company that provides garden mulch, does not work particularly well for me."

RH "This logo is an update of the old Standard logo and retains the original script. The 'S' has been simplified by the removal of a loopy flourish. The colors are suitably firey, and the whole is set against a black night sky. The white sparks are somewhat limply drawn and could have done with more power and drama. The Photoshop chamfer is unnecessary and will date quickly."

AW "A diagonal oval is uncommonly used, and it distinguishes this mark. The 'S' shape doesn't look right at its terminals—it is too wide for the rest of the letterforms. The 'a's and 'd's are the same shape—with and without an ascender—and they are poorly proportioned, being too fat at seven o'clock.

"The tail of the final 'd' is inelegantly joined on its underside with the yellow swash. And the space between the 'S' and the swash should be equivalent to the space between the swash and the baseline of the lowercase letters."

RH "Consistent use of the rounded type would give this logo more polish. The 'e' of 'ripe' has more to do with the edge of the apple than the rest of the word—a little more air here would help."

AW "Terrific color use!"

RH "Chocolates? Looks more like a surfing or tribal tattoo parlor logo to me."

RM "For some reason (and whether it was intentional or not) the illustration looks like it's been stretched from side to side. To prove it to myself, I opened the image in Photoshop, and, after squishing it, it definitely looks better square (or in about a 4:3 proportion)."

AW "The illustration is wonderful: chocolates made by a marsupial or baby sasquatch. But neither typeface has the least stylistic character in common with the illustration (though both lines are sized to match the width). And since the illustration kills, the type must accommodate it, not the other way around."

HARRIETTE'S
SONG

Creative firm
nealedesign
Wellington, New Zealand

Client
Cherish Jeweller, Ltd.

Industry
Retail, Jewelry

Creative firm
Rule29
Geneva, IL

Client
Harriette's Song

Industry
Nonprofit

 "Idiosyncratic letterforms add a vintage appeal to this design. The use of the rational geometry of the Din font for the byline, however—designed by the German Wilhelm Pischner and suggested by the German Standards Committee (Deutsches Institut für Normung, hence 'DIN') for use in official signage—has a cold 'Form IS Function' geometry that perhaps jars. A softer, more idiosyncratic sans would fit better."

 "Looks like a box of tissues, which isn't necessarily a bad thing."

 "A logo in the 'guitar made of words' tradition. Other alumni include The Monkees."

 "That the mark represents an entity that works on behalf of kids eases the feeling of corniness. The space above the top of the 'H' is exactly that wide to agree with which other space in the mark? And there are inconsistencies in the curve of the 'S' guitar body that either need to be cleaned up, or the rest of the guitar needs to be crafted a little more loosely to match."

Creative firm
Siquis
Baltimore, MD

Client
Earth Shoes

Industry
Footwear

 "A heart-shaped tree is a simple and effective idea, here limply executed. The trunk has been repeated on the ends of the 'E' and 'W,' weirdly at 90 degrees and upside down. The letters in 'WOOD' overlap, while those in 'FREE' don't—though the type is obviously intended to have a vernacular irregular bounce, these irregular effects generally look best if they look like they've been applied consistently to the logo as a whole. Regular irregularity!"

 "This playful logo has a number of things going in its favor. It has a strong balance of all graphic elements (you have to love it when a logo name is perfectly balanced with only four characters). The blocked-in color fields are simple and successful at conveying a tree-hugging theme. I would have loved to see this logo executed with the characters in old woodblock letterforms. It almost begs to have some sort of texture."

 "What is the ultimate way of showing 'no wood'? I'm thinking it would be through white space where the trunk would ordinarily be. Having said that, the only part that fights here is the 'WOOD FREE' type, which competes far too much with the lovely tree and more elegant green type."

Creative firm
Rome & Gold Creative
Albuquerque, NM

Client
Boba Tea Company

Industry
Tea Beverages

Creative firm
Kinesis, Inc.
Ashland, OR

Client
Red Snail

Industry
Online Retail

 "I sort of like the illustration, although I tend to get a fast-food or food court read. Seems appropriate for some smoothie or whipped drink rather than a tea-derived drink. The 'M' in 'COMPANY' seems to be the odd one out (too many sharp angles)."

 "A *'boba'* is a pearl of tapioca in a glass of tea—a bit of knowledge that may illuminate this illustration. The type has false small caps; we can tell because the weight of the initial letters ('B' and 'T') is bolder than the rest of the primary type ('OBA' and 'EA'). Making the smaller caps a little heavier is an easy repair in Illustrator."

 "The funny typeface and counterintuitive color shift make this otherwise rather plain illustration succeed."

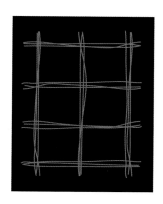

Creative firm
Underscore
London, UK

Client
Baby Dan

Industry
Retail

 "Gray plus a bright color is always a successful combination. The three elements in this mark—the tree illustration, the primary type, and the secondary type—have nothing much in common save for proximity."

"The tree could easily adopt the design feel of the primary type, which is at once organic and geometric. The secondary type could be replaced with another sans serif that has round—or at least rounder—letterforms, so it looks like it was matched with the display type in the name."

Creative firm
Watts Design
South Melbourne, Australia

Client
6 Acres Winery

Industry
Wine

 "As wineries shed their stuffy images, independent vintners are embracing a simpler, classy style. 6 Acres does this well with understated typography and a delicate illustration that works very well on a wine bottle."

 "Charming elements whose golden color joins them into a singular mark for a very small Australian winery."

Creative firm
Jeff Andrews Design
Salem, OR

Client
Fusion Juice

Industry
Restaurant, Food and Beverage

Creative firm
M3 Advertising Design
Las Vegas, NV

Client
Chronos / M3ad.com

Industry
Design, Promotional, Retail

 "I wish more attention had been given to the black internal areas, which are more open on the left than the right. The 'F' reads as an 'E' (a quick 'man in the street' test resolves issues like that), and the spacing between the 'F' and the 'U' and the 'U' and the 'S' is far wider than in the rest of the design. Black currant and lime colors are nice, though."

 "This is noteworthy for its successful alteration of the form of an 'S' so it agrees with those of a 'U' and an 'N.' There is a lot of random activity in this mark, one of which is the highlight on the dot, which should either be removed or echoed in the other green shape for consistency."

 "While designed clearly to evoke a mid-century modern Las Vegas feeling, I had a 'which one of these is not like the others' moment when my eyes rested on the bomb. Now, I would imagine someone who has survived a bomb attack might feel lucky, but the blithe reference to devastating weaponry could have been omitted."

 "This is a pastiche of existing pieces, compiled to evoke a WWII feeling for a retailer in Las Vegas. Shading helps define the background, and the north/south explosions in red are nicely translated for east/west use.

"On the other hand, relationships are not defined; these pieces just exist near each other. The scriptiness of 'Lucky' has been compromised by poor letter-to-letter spacing, which looks like very large typesetting rather than a whole word stylishly rendered."

Creative firm
rauhaus
Oshkosh, WI

Client
Oliver's Specialty Foods

Industry
Retail Specialty Foods

Creative firm
Glitschka Studios
Salem, OR

Client
Upper Deck Company—NFL License

Industry
Sports Collectibles

 "The concept, colors, and type choices work together very well here. Even the big apostrophe fits. The white hand with the aristocratic pinky adds a touch of humor to the logo and focuses our attention on the olive."

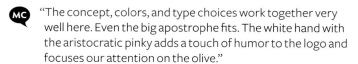 "Olive as i-dot— a simple idea, somewhat let down by a poor drawing of a hand with a broken little finger. Maybe it was designed by Harrison Ford after filming *Blade Runner.*"

 "Catching personality with few details is an art that this icon practices with panache. Seen small, the hat is the first read, and since it's a Bryant signature, that's almost all you need. But when you zoom in, there's lots more to love. The details of the gingham plaid in the hat and hat band, and the iconic profile make it seem like he's just left the room."

 "The execution of the check follows the contours of the hat very successfully, describing volume very simply."

"Good design is a lot like clear thinking made visual."

Edward Tufte

CHAPTER 4
Smart & Effective

Clever Solutions for Everyday Companies

Creative firm
Koch Creative Group
Wichita, KS

Client
Koch Industries, Inc.

Industry
Manufacturing

Creative firm
Fresh Oil
Pawtucket, RI

Client
Health Technology Services

Industry
Healthcare, IT

 "This marketing group will never need to raise their voices; their logo will do it for them. The fact that this megaphone needs its own stand makes it apparent that it's huge, which suggests the idea of marketing for large companies in a humorous way. The balance of positive and negative space and the simplicity of the illustration make this a very strong icon."

 "This is a well-judged execution that balances negative and positive space. The 'megaphone' to me more resembles a telescope—it's got a little viewfinder on the side, and the end looks like a lens—could it be that in telling us they can see the future, they forgot to see that the icon could be misinterpreted?"

 "A great concept for a business that 'gets the word out.' It's a simple execution but very effective."

 "Telescope, megaphone, or cannon? Any of the three is a strong message. Accurate representation is maybe less important than an abstraction of 'enlargement' or 'amplification.' There is an opportunity for a playful relationship between the two round shapes, the front of the megaphone and the bounding circle, that hasn't been exploited. And the craft of the object is not refined."

 "This whimsical mark communicates the idea of high-tech help for ailing healthcare computers with humor and style. The eye-catching colors and digital design are both hip and appropriate. I'll take two and call them in the morning."

 "The healthcare symbol—the snake curled around the staff—is designed to also resemble a printed circuit. A neat melding of the symbols for technology and health (though printed circuits are technically no longer cutting-edge)."

 "Healthcare plus IT services results in this iteration of the well-known Staff of Asclepius. Asclepius was a Greek physician in about 1200 BC and came to be revered as the God of Healing. The Staff of Asclepius is often confused with the two-snakes-on-a-rod-with-wings, which is the Caduceus, or wand of Hermes (Greek) or Mercury (Roman)."

Creative firm
Fresh Oil
Pawtucket, RI

Client
Rhode Runner

Industry
Retail, Footwear

Creative firm
Reactivity Studio
Austin, TX

Client
Austin Professional Landmen's Association

Industry
Oil and Land Procurement

 "This anchor is definitely not stuck in the mud. There's just enough gesture and whimsy in the illustration to make the point. It will work great on its own and also supports the play on words in the company name with additional humor."

 "A great example of how taking a familiar icon, in this case an anchor, and simply changing one element can lead to a very effective result."

 "This is a great play off of the company name. The use of highlights gives the anchor a feeling of strength and stability."

 "Rhode Island is known as 'the Ocean State,' and an anchor is part of the state seal, so a running anchor is a sensible mark for a running store there. This anchor has a certain dexterity and a very definite lightness on its feet."

 "Clip art–style illustration and retro type are deftly combined to create this wonderful seal. The balance of detail and boldness creates a sense of history without seeming boring or hidebound. I just KNOW these guys smoke cigars!"

 "The balance of this seal is perfect. All its elements are perfectly proportioned to help it get noticed."

 "Don't know what landmen are, but they sure were keen on having a timeless mark. Best part: the oil well/capital rotunda (Austin is the capital of Texas) combination with the star exploding out the top."

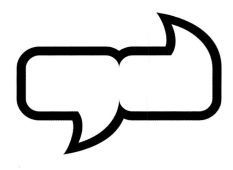

Creative firm
Reactivity Studio
Austin, TX

Client
Harvest Pest Control

Industry
Pest Control

Creative firm
Hardy Design
Anderson, SC

Client
Ligatures

Industry
Graphic Design, Web Publication

MC "This is an unsettling combination of images that conveys the company's business quite well, and the colors suggest the blend of agriculture and industry perfectly. I definitely don't want to find this guy at my next picnic!"

RM "A very clever idea. The colors speak well to the nature of the business. The lines creating the negative space are of a perfect weight that balances the logo nicely."

AW "There is a certain classicism to the split circle. This is a neat idea, but the scale of the corn kernels and husks is too fine for the line quality of the bug."

MC "This strong, slightly tech-feeling mark is a thoroughly appropriate application of two somewhat overused symbols. The simplicity is eye-catching, and the rendering is clean and powerful. I'm curious to see how the rest of the site stands up."

RH "The happy resemblance of speech balloons and speech marks has underpinned many logos. The curves in the 'tails' could be better, and the 'ruler and compass' corners need smoothing out but, other than that, a simple and effective, clean logo."

AW "A *ligature* is, in general, a thing used for tying something tightly, and in design, it is a character consisting of two or more joined letters. That this mark represents a design dialogue website explains the speech blurbs. The two points where the blurbs have been joined look too small and too pointy when compared with the two other points."

Creative firm
Refinery Design Company
Dubuque, IA

Client
Archiglass

Industry
Design

 "I'm having a craftsman 80s revival flashback here, and—oh my god—it's bright, but I love it!"

 "The fact that this logo is a photograph (or a convincing photoshop mock-up) adds a degree of verisimilitude and tactility that reflects the fine craftsmanship of the firm.

"The colors are slightly brash for a Mackintosh pastiche, though revival may not be the intent of the designer—other than the dot under the 'C,' the other letters more resemble geometric 70s Deco."

"Very Rennie—Mackintosh, I mean. Beautifully crafted, but I'm afraid the colors are a bit exaggerated for Rennie's liking. Still, the textures and highlights bring this mark to life."

Creative firm
Reactivity Studio
Austin, TX

Client
Sunrise Office Company

Industry
Office Supplies Retailer

"It's a tape dispenser sun! I love its simplicity and boldness. The type choice is perfect for its no nonsense, industrial boldness. It balances well with the huge black shape, and the use of color is just right."

"This combination of symbols makes great sense. Wish the dispenser, which seems rather clunky, looked more in tune with the proportion of the sun. The counterintuitive color assignment is a nice touch."

Creative firm
Reactivity Studio
Austin, TX

Client
Numb Popsicle Stand

Industry
Popsicle Retailer

Creative firm
Lloyds Graphics Design, Ltd.
Blenheim, New Zealand

Client
Manuka Hill Free Range Eggs

Industry
Food, Produce

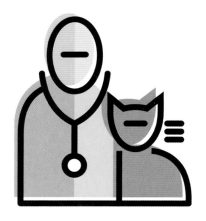

Creative firm
Noble and Associates
Springfield, MO

Client
Iams

Industry
Pet Care

Creative firm
Robison Creative Studios
Springfield, MO

Client
World Outreach

Industry
Nonprofit

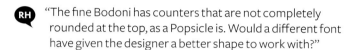

MC "This is a smart and witty use of negative space and color. I can't wait for summer so I can try one!"

RH "The fine Bodoni has counters that are not completely rounded at the top, as a Popsicle is. Would a different font have given the designer a better shape to work with?"

RM "This is fun and imaginative. It's smart, but I think a friendlier font would make it more effective."

AW "I happen to think Fudgsicles are the best of all flavors, so I'd have turned the 'u' upside down for an additional pop!"

MC "This is a wonderful, whimsical, personality-filled mark with type that doesn't have any of the same random joy. Why create such a great illustration and then use a typeface for the rest? I'm dying to see what the lettering would look like if the illustrator just kept going with a fatter line."

RH "Three eggs, neatly repeated. A hand-drawn texture to the linework of the illustration would add a homey touch—the current vector linework lacks character and reveals the mark's computer origins."

AW "Fabulous art! The old bugaboo of using a hand-lettered font—along with much too open spacing in the secondary type—hurts the bottom third of this mark. Fix the spacing in the second line by enlarging the type. Fix the precisely repeated 'handwritten' letters by replacing pieces from other characters for slight variations."

MC "This is a nice illustration that works well to communicate vets and pets. The two flat ends to the lines below the cat's head are the only places where the strokes aren't rounded. If they were either rounded or connected I'd be happier. The off-register color fills are a nice touch that give a casual feeling to the constrained line style."

RM "Single line weight logos can be pretty bulletproof. The things to look out for are the areas between lines when they get close, and where a line comes close but stops, like below the cat's head. Keep these areas in line, and these kind of logos can be successful. They also don't have a lot of character and usually feel very machine-made. Use when appropriate."

AW "Being 'off register' makes this mark. Anything that we think is 'normal' is an opportunity to be turned inside out for a disinctive logo."

MC "These hands seem like they're about to take off and fly away—an effect that enhances the 'angel' aspects of an outreach program. Unfortunately, the 'seen-it-a-thousand-times' aspect of these international symbol–style icons takes away from the message. If the hands were more unique and better related to the type style's not-quite-serif weight variations, this logo would be more memorable."

AW "That the hands form a 'W' is an almost hidden benefit. Would this not look far better if real hands had been photographed or scanned, and the high-contrast image distorted, as this pairing of antibacterial, generic icons has been?"

217

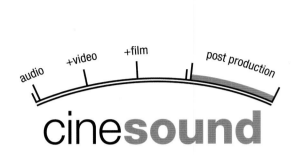

 Creative firm
Igility
Springfield, MO

Client
Igility

Industry
Online Software

 "DARIL" stands for
Data Asset Research
Information Library.

 "I'm not quite sure what's going on here, but I like it anyway. I love the business-guy icon with his sheaf of paper and juggling balls. I'm guessing the 'online software' has something to do with screen representation given the RGB colors? The type is odd but memorable and goes well with the icon's crisp corners and round curves, despite its much lighter weight."

"Is this fellow wearing swim fins? Neutralize the weird head and feet shapes to reduce visual static and enhance the contrast between gray guy and colored balls. The dot on the 'i' is too big, but not so big that it disagrees with the three balls on the tray: it is neither fish nor fowl. And it's spacing is too tight in relation to all other spacings in this mark."

Creative firm
Fauxkoi Design Company
Minneapolis, MN

Client
Cine Sound

Industry
Audio Production

 "The clever use of the gauge graphic communicates the company's capabilities with a touch of humor. Even in small applications, when the secondary type is too small to read, the gauge graphic will still convey meaning and support the memorability of the mark."

 "This logo does illustrate the process the company offers, and is thus very descriptive, almost giving a project timeline. Typographically, consistent font use (Helvetica) ensures cohesion."

 "This is a nice metaphor for showing the horsepower you will get when you use this company's services. This logo says 'works hard' and 'high energy.' Nicely done."

 "Refreshing lack of sound waves for a sound-related business. Touch of humor and realism make this a fine example."

MID *Atlantic* PRIME

Creative firm
Fauxkoi Design Company
Minneapolis, MN

Client
Mid Atlantic Prime

Industry
Financial

MC "This is a sophisticated mix of fonts that feels stately but still contemporary. The modified serifs are nicely handled and give the caps an updated feeling without losing credibility. However, the adjustment to extend the left side of the 'A' looks awkward for two reasons: the kink in the curve and the sudden lack of weight variation, neither of which matches the rest of the script."

RH "The x-height of the script is so very nearly the same as the serif cap height—it seems odd not to make them match exactly."

RM "It's very pretty, classy, and a bit masculine at the same time. The long curl on the 'A' has a subtle weird bend in it, but other than that, it's very conservative. This is appropriate for a financial company, and I can see very traditional uses for the logo."

AW "The typographic contrasts are so great in this mark that the word spaces are not necessary."

Creative firm
Ellen Bruss Design
Denver, CO

Client
The Oven Pizza é Vino

Industry
Restaurant

MC "This is a nice example of a containing shape that works as an icon, too. Allowing the type to float inside the shape and align with the handle creates a nice balance between minimalism and whimsy."

RM "This makes sense as a full locked-up logo but I hope there are other treatments that allow for readability at smaller sizes. But the large pizza paddle can be an ownable shape for them."

AW "Simple, no-nonsense approach that promises unadorned pie and wine, despite the elongated pizza peel."

skate. surf. live.

Creative firm
Jeff Andrews Design
Salem, OR

Client
Rogue River Boardshop

Industry
Sports, Manufacturing, Entertainment

Creative firm
DogStar
Birmingham, AL

Client
Birmingham Greenways

Industry
Urban Park Development

Creative firm
BBK Studio
Grand Rapids, MI

Client
Grand Rapids Art Museum

Industry
Museum, Art, Culture

Creative firm
Misha Birmele Designer Graphics
Pasadena, CA

Client
Southern Adventist University

Industry
Nonprofit

Rogue River BOARDSHOP

MC "This is a nice, clean application of Magneto script, but the space between the final 'e' and 'r' is a bit too open. The off-center 'BOARDSHOP' in light caps is a nice touch that emphasizes the weight of the script and frame. The tagline is so small it's almost invisible."

RH "The tagline is (skate, surf, live) way too small."

RM "The badge is a great way to communicate 'strong and sturdy.' I'd like to move the word 'BOARDSHOP' over to line up flush right. It is causing too much tension in the logo."

AW " 'BOARDSHOP' and tagline are the same typeface but differ in size, position, and caps/lowercase form. Reduce their contrasts from three to two or one and gain design unity. Reducing their contrasts will also let 'Rogue River' become more prominent, as it deserves."

MC "This clever conjunction of symbols works well to communicate the idea of greenways. The 'toes' have the not-quite-round irregularity of stones and other natural objects. This logo makes me want to walk in the grass barefooted."

RH "A foot and a leaf: a simple but effective illustration of Greenways—green urban walking routes."

AW "What a lovely idea: combining leaf with toes to get a nature walkway. But this looks like a found leaf icon was given five toes that are at once too small and too pudgy for such a long, elegant foot. Put another way, what is specifically right about this particular combination of foot and toe shapes?"

GRAM

MC "This is a design that does a pretty good job of staying out of its own way. Aside from a few letterspacing issues, the beefy weight and simple color palette should allow this logo to make a statement without overwhelming the art it's promoting."

RM "This is very smart on so many levels for being very simple. A logo for a museum must rely on minimal identity. A museum's strength and identity come from what they exhibit and how they exhibit. They literally are the blank wall to hang the canvas, so their logo and identity need to be able to accommodate any size of canvas."

AW "Spacing letterforms starts by identifying the trickiest pair. In this case, it is the 'RA.' The other pairs must be spaced to look equivalently distant. The 'AM' is measurably equal: the spaces at the baseline between the 'RA' and the 'AM' are the same. But there is less 'R' at its right edge than there is 'M' at its left edge, so the 'M' looks closer to the 'A.' Compensate by nudging the 'M' a tiny bit further away.

"In comparison to the 'RA' spacing, the 'GR' pairing is simply too tight. There appears to be much more white between the 'RA' than between the 'GR.' "

MC "Crown logos are everywhere, so it's great to see a fresh take on an old standby. The interlocking people are beautifully executed. They're obviously figures but also easily readable as a crown. The metaphor isn't at all strained. The visual double entendre is perfectly appropriate for a Christian service organization."

AW "A crown made of people helping—or at least interacting with—each other. This is a tasty solution for a Christian community service program."

Creative firm
Dotzero Design
Portland, OR

Client
Trullenque Plantaciones & Jardins

Industry
Landscape Design, Gardening

 "I love the retro feeling of the bold condensed caps used here. The pointy 'N,' unique 'Q,' and desaturated color palette make it feel like a logo with a lot of history. The organic plaque shape and rays suggest the sun or sheafs of wheat. It's so wholesome, it's almost edible."

 "This is a Spanish gardening business that asked not to have plants in their logo. What they got is great fun and satisfactorily disguises their industry."

Creative firm
Ellen Bruss Design
Denver, CO

Client
The Press Coffee Company

Industry
Restaurant

 "This is a great use of wonky, computer-traced script. The big fat beans and eccentric squiggles actually work pretty well here to communicate a sense of casual play. The two 's's in 'press' and two 'f's and 'e's in 'coffee' should be more different from each other so the logo feels less like a typeface and more like coffee spilled on the table."

 "Autotracing scanned art gives rise to a very distictive vector roughness, seen here to good effect. Like all such computer tricks, it may date quickly, however."

 "Very interesting typography, but the beans are a bit too much. This is very warm and playful. I like that the coffee cup illustration can work on its own and still integrate with the full lockup."

 "Looking beyond the highly decorative letterforms, this mark uses space and size quite well. The cup's crookedness makes a huge contribution."

Mosquito

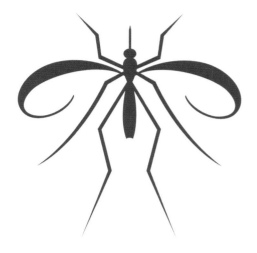

Creative firm
Fauxkoi Design Company
Minneapolis, MN

Client
Pocket Hercules

Industry
Printing

 "This is a wonderful logo. It combines elegantly simple typography with a subtle and humorous icon that communicates both blood and ink at the same time. I get the point!"

 "Overprinting the 'CMY' reflects the familiar printing process. No 'K,' however—instead we have a gray, possibly 50 percent 'K'? This may be so as not to swamp the small droplets, which could benefit from being larger. The 'M' has been thoughtfully designed to reflect the round lowercase forms and eliminate the usual diagonals, which would jar in this context."

 "This is a logo that simply explains what the company does. This company's customers (especially designers) would quickly recognize it and appreciate the clean logo as opposed to the usually cumbersome logos that most printers have."

 "Ink as blood! The spacing of these particular lightweight letterforms produces a nice rhythm of interior and exterior space."

Creative firm
Fauxkoi Design Company
Minneapolis, MN

Client
Pocket Hercules

Industry
Printing

 "As much as I LOVE this icon, it seems a bit literal and unnecessary next to the elegance of the lettering on the left. That aside, this is a wonderful illustration that combines gracefulness and pointy tension. It's making me itch just looking at it!"

 "While this is a terrific mosquito, if it was meant to be used with the type element at left, there is a disconnect in shared design attributes. Easily solved by, for example, changing the type's gray color to this blood red. This adds something interesting to the word logo: primary colors being wrung from blood."

Creative firm
Give Something Back International Logo
San Francisco, CA

Client
University of California, Davis

Industry
Education

MC "This series of icons is very well executed. The positioning and use of negative space is well considered and consistent. My issue is with the originality of the concept in the first place. Both the hands and many of the other symbols are so overused that they've lost any emotional impact. These feel like international wayfinding symbols more than icons for a campus that cares."

RM "A family of related logos have to have an overarching design concept that holds them all together—here it's the hand, symbolizing the 'helping hand' of the 'Caring for the Campus' theme of the University of California campus facilities group. Color coding provides differentiation, and care has been taken to align the elements in each palm with the hand itself."

AW "Fine generic symbols, if a bit too scrubbed of character. How can the University of California 'own' this series of corporate-looking symbols? Is there a way to incorporate existing iconography into this new set? Doesn't 'caring' suggest a personal touch? These represent robotic caring, if there is such a thing."

Creative firm
Solak Design Company
New Hartford, CT

Client
Upward Bound Basketball Camp

Industry
Sports

 "I like the sketchy quality of this mark, but I LOVE what's left out. Leaving out the rest of the circle allows the lines to seem light and optimistic, almost as if the arrow has wings and is about to take off."

 "An arrow pointing 'onward and upward' is a tried and tested logo design cliché, but one that can still be fresh if given the right treatment. Here, the hand-drawn, scratchy quality of the execution gives it an appropriate edgy dynamism.

"Arrows in this usage generally point up to the right, presumably to mimic a graph that reads left to right, a convention this design bucks. Do countries who write right to left also flip their graphs and so use arrows rising to the left in their designs? It's an intriguing thought."

 "The loose line work and lack of color is very effective in conveying the serious nature of the camp. The not-so-prominent arrow is a nice surprise."

 "The scratchy quality of this mark is refreshing and shows 'work in progress,' like the kids who attend this basketball camp. Would the lettering dare to have the same drawn quality?"

Creative firm
Lloyds Graphics Design, Ltd.
Blenheim, New Zealand

Client
ViaStrada

Industry
Professional

 "Tarmac-gray and road marking–yellow are appropriate colors for this company offering expertise in road management, planning and design to maximize road safety and better traffic flow.

"Repeating the 'I' to create a lane division marking is an idea I've seen before—I have a vehicle licensing reminder here on my desk that uses the same concept—but the execution is simple and neat. The missing crossbars on the 'A's should be consistent—why does the bold 'A' need a crossbar when the others don't?"

 "The use of type and color are right on target here. The use of the bold weight vs. lighter weight is very effective in separating the words."

 "Color, weight contrast, and spacing are all very good. Two things to consider: the difference in crossbars of the 'A's, and the yellow dashes would really love to interact with the secondary type rather than bang into 'TRAFFIC.'"

Creative firm
BBK Studio
Grand Rapids, MI

Client
1to3.org

Industry
Environmental Sustainability

Creative firm
zumablue!
Westlake Village, CA

Client
Stonroc

Industry
Wholesale

Creative firm
BBK Studio
Grand Rapids, MI

Client
VMF

Industry
Finance

Creative firm
BBK Studio
Grand Rapids, MI

Client
Central Michigan Paper (CMP)

Industry
Paper Distributor

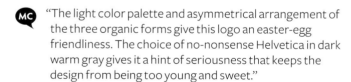

MC "The light color palette and asymmetrical arrangement of the three organic forms give this logo an easter-egg friendliness. The choice of no-nonsense Helvetica in dark warm gray gives it a hint of seriousness that keeps the design from being too young and sweet."

RH "Pebbles—that's the immediate image this logo evokes. Natural shades of green and blue support the company's business, which is promoting sustainability by helping organizations and individuals find sustainable products and services."

AW "Eggs or stones? Either way, excellent negative space between them and the type."

MC "There's a wonderful, sophisticated, European feeling to this logo, created by the off-center sans-serif type, the elongated rectangle aligned to the square, and the tilted elliptical shape of the 'stone.' The transparent waves of color give the icon a feeling of translucency, depth, and movement that keeps the entire design from being overly simple and bland."

RH "An off-center type treatment and extended font recalls a modernist 60s-influenced heritage."

RM "The manner in which the object breaks the bounds of the square creates a nice energy flow. The color combinations give the logo a retro feel, while the mark itself is current."

AW "Delicious use of color tints and screens in the illustration. Space is consciously used in the placement of the name. Umlauts, the diacritical marks over the 'o's, move the sound of the vowels to the front of the mouth, but visually make this look Germanesque."

RM "Very clever typography, but it runs the risk of being too clever. Will non-designers get a 'V,' 'M,' and 'F' out of it, or just 'MF'? I trust that the 'VMF' is known in its market and that the entire brand built explains the full name. But technically, this is solid."

AW "Abstraction is the act of removing unnecessary parts so an underlying truth is revealed. It is tricky to get three letters to merge into a single mark; the essence of each letter must be retained.

"The 'F' comes through best of all. The problematic letters are the 'V' and 'M,' which here are skewed too much toward fidelity to the 'V.' The 'M' has been condensed in service to the 'V' and 'F.'"

RH "A logo with a sense of fun—unusual for this kind of business. I'd like to see the feet designed to more resemble folded paper, and a forward lean would have imparted some kinetic energy."

RM "An unusually humorous solution—but memorable for that very reason."

AW "Alignment of eyeglasses and midpoint of type glues these parts together. The bent back corner is too obvious a symbol of paper. Perhaps deleting the top horizontal rule entirely would be a subtler solution—and it would activate the white space."

Creative firm
Watts Design
South Melbourne, Australia

Client
Tom Freeman

Industry
Underwater Surveyor

Creative firm
Watts Design
South Melbourne, Australia

Client
Vicki Freeman

Industry
Accountant

Creative firm
Lloyds Graphics Design Ltd.
Blenheim, New Zealand

Client
Havelock Slipway

Industry
Marine

Creative firm
Watts Design
South Melbourne, Australia

Client
Spicers Paper

Industry
Paper

MC "This icon really measures up! It's a quick read as the intended visual pun, plus it has some wonderful historical resonance. The nautilus shell's logarithmic spiral was thought to manifest the ideal proportions of the golden mean and was an early symbol for perfection in measurement and proportion. It's the perfect shell to use as a symbol for an underwater tape measure."

RH "Two at once. Another nice use of photography as icon. Now that most business is done via the Web, the old limitations of color and print are becoming less of an issue. Designers are embracing solutions that would have been tricky to implement in the days when limited color print was the primary medium in which a logo would appear."

AW "Lovely idea, but the execution is a bit off. The shell should be bigger for that tape (or the tape should be smaller for that shell), and the way the tape enters the shell is unconvincing. With photography's realism, these match-ups become much more significant. What is right about this length of tape being shown? Probably less is better—just enough to make the point."

HAVELOCK **SLIPWAY**

RH "A little more kerning on the 'WAY' of 'SLIPWAY' would add finesse."

AW "It helps to have an extraordinarily good name with which to work. The illustration is a fine combination of strength of 'boat' and liquidity of 'water.'"

MC "This is a great mark for a bean counter with a sense of humor. The photo-real treatment adds an additional sense of whimsy to the already amusing 1-plus-1-equals-three idea. This accountant might even make accounts payable seem less hideous than usual."

RH "An excellent use of photography, and a fresh yet immediately comprehensible solution for the dullest of clients, the accountant. Sterling stuff. One tweak—the plus and the equals are a wee bit weedy and would get lost at small sizes."

AW "An accountant with a sense of humor and a questionable sense of mathematics. Why are the three beans slightly reduced in scale?"

SNOWCARD

MC "This is a nice use of a dingbat. You don't get the detail of the snowflake until you zoom in, but even small, the lettering feels light and fluffy in spite of its digital design."

RH "The hexagonal shape of the snowflake leads to a hexagonal grid-based typeface. An interesting excercise that lends itself more successfully to some letters than to others—for example, the 'D' is narrower than the other characters."

AW "The danger of designing letterforms on a grid (an 'external space-arranging construct') is that the grid will impose itself in a way that is hurtful to the letters and their spacing. Here the design is affected by being forced onto a grid that is too coarse and limiting at seven units high. A finer grid would provide more options, but the little snowflake icons would become even tinier."

Creative firm
Rome & Gold Creative
Albuquerque, NM

Client
Native Landscapes

Industry
Landscaping

 "This logo has a wonderful handmade, cared-for feeling that seems completely right for the business. The imperfections in the illustration and even the subtle shadow give it a touch of reality. The type choice is also a good one. The spaces following the caps are a bit too open in both words, but other than that, I dig it!"

 "Warmth expressed in the rendering of the shovel is echoed in the type choice."

Creative firm
A3 Design
Charlotte, NC

Client
Bryant & Duffey Optometrists

Industry
Optometrists

 "What a great way to use the perfect gift of letters! The square shapes give it a slightly trendy feeling while still reminding us of reading glasses and old-time spectacles. What does the type look like? I hope it's just as good."

 "I've seen many logos based on glasses—they do offer great opportunities for designers. It's, therefore, difficult to do in a new way. This is unlike any I've seen before and is a fresh take on an old idea. The 'bd' initials are an absolute gift, and the square frames give it a contemporary edge that round frames would just not have."

 "Great. Wonder what the alternate interpretations look like? This basic idea is almost infinitely permutable—as many variations as there are frames on their shelves."

Women's Business Lunch

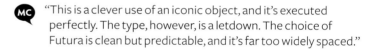

Creative firm
Wibye Advertising & Graphic Design
London, UK

Client
The Women's Company

Industry
Business, Networking

MC "I love the icon/illustration. Its casual, squiggly style works great to underscore the whimsical lipstick mark. The type is really underwhelming though and seems completely overpowered by the mark."

RH "A great concept. Idea-led logos are some of the most memorable, and this is no exception. If I had to quibble, I'd point out that the glass is somewhat crudely drawn; the stem especially could be more elegantly curved."

RM "The manner in which the illustration has a 'sketch' quality, combined with the lipstick on the glass, gives a sense of casualness and fun with this group. This logo is very inviting. The use of color on both the lipstick and the type is a great way to tie the logo's purpose together."

AW "Simple, uncluttered, and expressive."

Creative firm
Wibye Advertising & Graphic Design
London, UK

Client
FashionWorks

Industry
Charity, Fashion

MC "This is a clever use of an iconic object, and it's executed perfectly. The type, however, is a letdown. The choice of Futura is clean but predictable, and it's far too widely spaced."

RH "This is a great example of when to use a photograph—the beautiful idiosyncrasies of the bent wire would be much more difficult to reproduce using a graphic or an illustration. The type, though weighted to match the wire, looks very 80s in its wide spacing and choice of font (Futura)."

RM "This is one of those logos that makes you think, 'Why didn't I think of that?' It is a wonderfully clever idea. The use of sans-serif type and weight is a perfect choice."

AW "Sometimes we see ideas that are so well conceived, they look obvious. This is such an idea. Wonderful use of natural materials and minimal typography acting in a secondary role."

Creative firm
Greteman Group
Wichita, KS

Client
Kansas Aviation Museum

Industry
Aviation Museum

 "This is a nearly flawless icon. I may be biased because I love everything having to do with flying, but I try never to let passion interfere with good design judgment.

"Everything here has been deftly considered, from the Deco-influenced style that relates to the museum building, to the relationship of line weight, negative space, and angle alignment. There's one really subtle curve issue where the two larger, inside-facing curls wrap around near the tail, but other than that, it's perfect!"

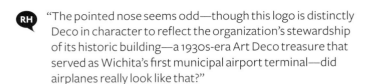 "The pointed nose seems odd—though this logo is distinctly Deco in character to reflect the organization's stewardship of its historic building—a 1930s-era Art Deco treasure that served as Wichita's first municipal airport terminal—did airplanes really look like that?"

"This mark for the Kansas Aviation Museum uses their historic 1930s Art Deco building at the Wichita airport. The power of this artwork suggests the type should play a secondary role."

Creative firm
Firebelly Design
Chicago, IL

Client
Faith in Place

Industry
Nonprofit

 "This is an very nice icon/illustration. I didn't notice the people until I enlarged it a little, but the surprise is nice. It might read better at small sizes if the heads were a touch larger. The icon is so nice, it deserves better type. It takes some sensitivity and possibly some delicate type customization to work with the curled final serifs on the lowercase 'a's and 't.'

"It might be better to choose another font with a similar feeling, like Egyptian, that can be spaced tighter because it doesn't have those issues."

 "Though typographically weak due to the old 'word-spacing-bigger-than-the-leading' bugbear, the illustration is a cleverly executed combination of people and trees. The long 'legs' resemble trunks, and their rough-hewn character adds a friendly and original finish. The leaves all emanate from the heads, lending the logo a distinct dynamism."

 "Excellent illustration for an outfit that brings congregations, clean energy and farming together. Clarendon is an equally excellent typeface, but default letter and word spacing was used, creating inconsistencies at display sizes."

FRESH OIL

Thinking Cap

Creative firm
Fresh Oil
Pawtucket, RI

Client
Fresh Oil

Industry
Design

 "This is a clever icon that goes well with the stencil-style type, but it feels a bit small in relation to the type shown here. I love the idea of oil-sprouting leaves; it's a bit like reverse evolution, or maybe reverse geology."

RH "Leaves, a symbol of all things fresh and natural, sprout from an industrial icon, the oil can. An intriguing combination."

RM "This logo is effective because it incorporates two objects that don't usually go together but does a great job in combining them."

AW "The oil can looks too small: its handle stroke width should match the letters beneath, and the spacing within the handle should equal the gaps in the stencil letters."

Creative firm
TOKY Branding + Design
St. Louis, MO

Client
Thinking Cap

Industry
Marketing, Research

 "This is a fun concept and a fairly good execution. There are a few details that, if fixed, would really make it smart. The cap is a bit clunky in its thick to thin transitions; it would be nice to have some of its thins relate to the thins in the type."

"There are a few letterspacing issues: the spaces between the 'T' and 'h,' and 'k' and 'i' are too open. The type choice is nice—very academic in feeling."

RH "A great name for a company. The hat is centered over the type, which shows attention to the overall balance. The hat itself seems to lack symmetry, however."

Creative firm
M3 Advertising Design
Las Vegas, NV

Client
Alternative Management

Industry
Office Management, Nonprofit

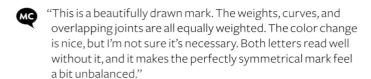 "This is a beautifully drawn mark. The weights, curves, and overlapping joints are all equally weighted. The color change is nice, but I'm not sure it's necessary. Both letters read well without it, and it makes the perfectly symmetrical mark feel a bit unbalanced."

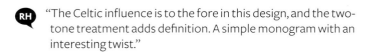 "The Celtic influence is to the fore in this design, and the two-tone treatment adds definition. A simple monogram with an interesting twist."

"Black, white, and a delicious woody brown joined with a tasteful 'AM' letterform blendation. Nothing needs to be adjusted."

Creative firm
Blacktop Creative
Kansas City, MO

Client
Style Boutique

Industry
Fashion

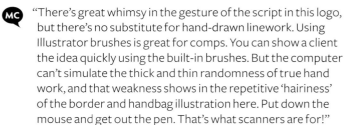 "There's great whimsy in the gesture of the script in this logo, but there's no substitute for hand-drawn linework. Using Illustrator brushes is great for comps. You can show a client the idea quickly using the built-in brushes. But the computer can't simulate the thick and thin randomness of true hand work, and that weakness shows in the repetitive 'hairiness' of the border and handbag illustration here. Put down the mouse and get out the pen. That's what scanners are for!"

"A spot-on execution of this kind of logo—casual, wonky, and fun. The loopy border is an Illustrator brush effect, however, so it lacks verisimilitude."

"Tasty and sweet. The texture was applied to all strokes equally and well and the color use—two percentages on one color—is simplified. Still, the overall result looks a touch generic. Maybe it's the bland name?"

territory management system

GREEN VALENTINE
LEARNING THAT ENGAGES

Creative firm
Chris Green
Shelby Township, MI

Client
Car.com

Industry
Automotive Services

Creative firm
Watts Design
South Melbourne, Australia

Client
Green Valentine

Industry
Legal Management

 "I love the energy in the Tiddlywinks icon. It is nicely drawn, and the subtle shading in the discs adds a nice sense of dimension. The initials seem to be spaced a bit too low, but their weight works nicely with the icon. The secondary type feels a bit like an afterthought."

 "Three fine ingredients with little that connects them. But, being a sucker for diagrammatic process, I am eager to see the sizes adjusted to look less random and more purposeful—perhaps by sharing a common width."

 "This is a nice use of a woodcut illustration to underscore the concept. The fact that the designer hasn't tried to make the heart more visible and resisted making it green demonstrates wonderful restraint. You read the tree first, and the heart magically appears when seen in conjunction with the word 'VALENTINE.' I like that the designer is giving his audience some credit for intelligence and not trying to hit us over the head."

 "It could also be read as one tree being split in half down the middle..."

 " 'Closure' is needed by the viewer to see the heart shape, which is an effective way to cause the viewer's involvement. The negative shapes under the branches don't contribute any meaning to this mark, which is a missed opportunity."

Creative firm
Design 446
Manasquan, NJ

Client
Winemiller Press

Industry
Printing

 "This logo is a great example of how a whole lot of nicely set and arranged type can hang together without needing lots of boxes and containing shapes. The central seal with the dragon is a great focal point, and the restrained color palette really makes this hang together. It has the elegance of a wine label, and I would expect their products to be exactly as high quality as they claim."

 "Thank goodness only one type family was used, or else this would be quite a tutti-frutti solution. There is a clear mini-mum repro size before serious loss of legibility kicks in. On the other hand, this may be the finest grain logo in this book, so its soft spot may also be its strongest characteristic."

Creative firm
Timber Design Company
Indianapolis, IN

Client
Lars Lawson

Industry
Design

 "This logo gives me the feeling that this would be a no-nonsense design firm. The backwoods icon's primitive simplicity suggests Davey-Crockett resourcefulness and works well with the pragmatic typeface. I wouldn't expect a lot of subtlety from these guys, but they look like they'd work hard."

"Liquorice Allsorts are doing stunt double duty here—the real logs didn't like the look of that axe."

 "This is great fun—and not at all an expected solution. How to get three elements—the illustration, the primary, and the secondary type—to become a stronger single entity? Close up the horizontal spacing."

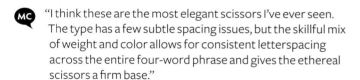

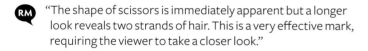

Creative firm
5Seven
San Francisco, CA

Client
Ryan Thomas Hair Studio

Industry
Retail, Cosmetics

MC "I think these are the most elegant scissors I've ever seen. The type has a few subtle spacing issues, but the skillful mix of weight and color allows for consistent letterspacing across the entire four-word phrase and gives the ethereal scissors a firm base."

RM "The shape of scissors is immediately apparent but a longer look reveals two strands of hair. This is a very effective mark, requiring the viewer to take a closer look."

AW "Weight contrast in type is marvelously interpreted and echoed in the illustration. This mark suggests artistry, which is what a fine salon really sells. Well, that plus the hope of looking better. Beautiful."

Creative firm
Blacktop Creative
Kansas City, MO

Client
Durham School Services

Industry
Transportation

MC "This logo is conceptually appropriate, as well as well drawn. Making a badge-style shield suggests the security of a police or sheriff's badge, while including the rounded rectangles and banners gives it a friendly, retro 40s feeling that softens the message."

RH "This logo should be accompanied by a booming voice akin to a Hollywood blockbuster voice-over... 'Road...to... EXCELLENCE!!!'"

AW "I think there is intentional humor in this mark. The tiny school bus with the flapping stop sign sitting atop a very impressive, very aggressive shield is too much of a contrast to be accidental. And speaking of contrast, are four type-faces for four words really necessary? More similarity will produce more elegance."

Creative firm
Fresh Oil
Pawtucket, RI

Client
Cowesett Inn

Industry
Restaurant

Creative firm
Jeff Kern Design
Springfield, MO

Client
Monroe County Martial Arts

Industry
Martial Arts

Creative firm
Robison Creative Studios
Springfield, MO

Client
High Street Baptist Church

Industry
Religion

Creative firm
Lloyds Graphics Design, Ltd.
Blenheim, New Zealand

Client
Adventure Sports

Industry
Sportswear, Active Wear, Outdoor Activities Retailer

MC "This is a very well-crafted and executed logo as far as all the details are concerned. There's nothing really wrong here, except that there's just too much going on. The designer has managed to put in so much detail that we lose sight of the goal. The final effect feels heavy, mechanical, and overwhelming, more appropriate for a mechanic or a machine shop than an inn or a restaurant."

RH "A 'let's throw in the kitchen sink' logo: ribbons, detailing, illustrations, shadows; it's very well executed, and does communicate a certain craftsmanship, tradition, and heritage, but is in need of an original concept. Maybe that means it's a perfect fit for the venue! Also, the angled bottles look somewhat contrived."

MC "Finally, a smart and funny use of the ubiquitous house symbol! The chimney doubling as a bo stick is pretty amusing, too. I would be tempted to try lowering the head a bit, but it might reduce the quick read on the house."

RM "This is smart, effective, and pretty funny. Great concept, but I'm not comfortable with the head balancing on the tip. Overall, I'm sure it gets them a lot of laughs and business."

AW "The head should relate to the roof exactly as the buckle relates to the negative space immediately beneath it. Otherwise, a delight."

RM "Illustrations of the actual business for a logo can be very effective at being recognizable and look very established. The building has a few flaws that keep it from being solid, but the type just isn't even close to holding up its part. But they're on the right track."

AW "I read 'TAHITI' in this mark. When a mark is thought to be 'too busy,' it means there are unresolved contrasts. A few here are the pointiness of the steeple vs. the square-ended lines, the round dot amid the angularity, and the round-ended porch/roofline amidst the square-ended lines. The contrast of this typeface with this illustration is profound, yet its size is quite deliberate."

RH "Binoculars, with two views—sea and land adventure—sum up the core market of this long-established retailer of high-quality outdoor clothing, equipment, and sportswear."

AW "Stencil-like gaps in the infinity symbol and the water artwork unify art with type. The road/mountain art doesn't quite capture that stencil effect but can be easily tweaked. I think the just-barely-off-horizontal 'ADVENTURE' is more interesting than the definitely-off-horizontal 'SPORTS' because it shows danger and risk."

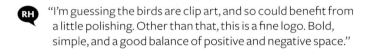

Creative firm
Reactivity Studio
Austin, TX

Client
Scott Birds

Industry
Bird Feed, Grooming Products Retailer

RH "I'm guessing the birds are clip art, and so could benefit from a little polishing. Other than that, this is a fine logo. Bold, simple, and a good balance of positive and negative space."

RM "Smart use of type and negative space. The illustrations are not too detailed, so things can hold up at any size."

AW "Conscious contrast of bold, stocky letterform and delicate, white birds."

Creative firm
TOKY Branding + Design
St. Louis, MO

Client
Pulitzer Foundation for the Arts

Industry
Arts

MC "The swirl of ink used here to connote water has the grace of a sume-i character and is integrated beautifully with the industrial sans-serif caps—Din is one of my favorites. The designer resisted the urge to clean things up and left random spatters and blobs that enhance the feeling of artistic authenticity."

RH "A beautiful, polished execution that has just the right amount of interaction between image and type. My only comment would be that rather than water, it looks like ink—maybe because of the color. Reversing the image or adding a hint of blue may help. Other than that, a great logo."

RM "This logo is a great combination of organic and sans-serif type. The lack of color is refreshing. It would almost be too obvious to have blue in this mark."

AW "Excellent interaction of image and letterforms: the letters are dominated by the imagery over the 'A' and the 'T,' and the image is dominated by the letterforms behind the 'W,' 'E,' and 'R.'"

Creative firm
Reactivity Studio
Austin, TX

Client
Ecology Center

Industry
Environmental Organization

 "An elegantly executed combination of birds and a tree that manages to also work as a beautiful rococo letterform."

 "This is one of a series, each using the baroque quality of this letter 'E' to great advantage. The variations in these three symbols are unified by scale, line weight, and curve shape. A system is clearly evident."

WOMEN AND GIRLS
FOUNDATION

Creative firm
Velocity Design Works
Winnipeg, Canada

Client
Carbon Interactive

Industry
Software, Technical

 "Here we have a piece of hand-drawn type that displays some of the visual glitches that professional type designers would iron out. Even in very 'ruler and compass' fonts such as Din, there is a lot of subtle redrawing to ensure the correct visual harmony.

"Here, the 'n' is too wide in comparison to the 'o,' even though the radius of the curve is the same. The 'n's larger counter (internal white space) is the cause of this optical illusion, and to correct this, the 'n' should be slightly narrower.

"The joins of the straight elements to the curved elements should be smoothed—rather than joining a semicircle directly to a line, a subtle straightening curve that flows into the line looks more elegant. Both these effects can be added without destroying the overall geometry of the design."

 "The effect of the 'carbon' lettering is great. But there is nothing that relates the primary and secondary type. They contrast in typeface, size, case, color, weight, and position. They relate only by proximity, but that's a default condition. It is useful to consider how few design relationships can be absent before a design can be considered a random assembly."

Creative firm
Fitting Group
Pittsburgh, PA

Client
Women and Girls Foundation

Industry
Nonprofit

 "The two point sizes used in the type give a subtle emphasis—possibly too subtle. The 'W' reminds me of the Wonder Woman chest emblem. Overall, a well-executed logo showing a balance of line weights."

 "The 'W' and 'G' are plainly there, but you get the pair of 'f's for free. 'F' as in 'female.' Having said that, I think the metallic sheen and rather macho letterform shapes with the wings are more professional wrestling and motorcycle manufacturer than social justice."

Creative firm
TOKY Branding + Design
St. Louis, MO

Client
Grand Center

Industry
Arts District Association, Nonprofit

 "Bright colors contrasted with black here definitely suggest both art and life. Deft letterspacing means that the four-letter word is the same width as the three."

 "Crossword puzzle solutions—using letters or words for double duty—are usually stale and unimaginative. This one works because it reveals additional meaning."

Creative firm
TOKY Branding + Design
St. Louis, MO

Client
Appistry

Industry
Computer Software

 "The op-art effect suggests moving toward a focus—a general, but effective solution."

 "This variation on a familiar op-art theme uses progressive angles and shading to affect the blurry, dimensional first impression."

Creative firm
Eye Design Studio
Charlotte, NC

Client
AIGA Charlotte

Industry
Nonprofit

AIGA, the professional association
for design, Charlotte chapter, holds a
morning meet-up event called BuzZ
at a local café. The event concept is to
have conversations over coffee, so the
icon represents that stylistically.

Creative firm
Eye Design Studio
Charlotte, NC

Client
Eye Design Studio

Industry
Design

Creative firm
Eye Design Studio
Charlotte, NC

Client
Pace Development, Inc.

Industry
Residential Community, Real Estate

Creative firm
Storm Corporate Design
Auckland, New Zealand

Client
WTG - Working Together

Industry
Social Organization

RH "I didn't spot the coffee cups until I read the explanation; possibly changing the color inside the cups to a brown may help matters. Other than that, a neat and balanced execution."

AW "The designer's statement says, in part, 'The Charlotte chapter (of the AIGA) holds a morning meet-up event at a local café.' Knowing this changes the mark's impression from mere Astrisk design to a near-illustration."

RH "The 'e' is not immediately apparent, but the execution is well balanced, and the line weights are generally consistent. The black line around the 'e' appears thinner than the white lines, however—it may benefit from being heavier."

AW "It took a few moments to see the negative space 'e,' but it makes a huge difference: the wings' details are drawn at the same width as the 'e.'"

RH "The spread of the serifs of the 'W' reflects the spread of the roots of the tree above where they meet the ground. A well-observed juxtaposition."

AW "The tree is centered over the 'W,' making this an asymmetrical (read: dynamic) design."

AW "This mark symbolizes two aspects of Islam: the square represents the Kabah in Mecca, and the dots represent Muslims walking around it. Even without knowing that, the design consistencies—the square's size is equal to the cap height of 'WTG,' and the type size is the same throughout—make this look like a well-organized entity."

Creative firm
Rome & Gold Creative
Albuquerque, NM

Client
Amigo Fiel

Industry
Humanitarian

 "This is a great concept, but the hammers are illustrated so literally that the heart gets lost. Simplifying the hammer icons and reducing the proportion of the handles would emphasize the heart and create a stronger mark."

 "The hammer is a practical and robust symbol, and it gives this clever logo its unique character, very unlike the somewhat airy and worthy solutions that commissions like this usually produce. Combined with the heart, this logo exudes strength and compassion at the same time—no easy feat."

 "Building plus love equals this simple and charming mark for an organization that builds homes for the homeless."

Creative firm
Addis Creson
Berkeley, CA

Client
Intel

Industry
High-Tech

 "The repeated rhythm of the letterforms is combined with hot colors to produce a dynamic whole."

 "Careful spacing and even color steps make four elements look like one."

Creative firm
Eye Design Studio
Charlotte, NC

Client
Warehouse 242

Industry
Church

 "Marvelous to see a counterintuitive mark for a church. The code in the 'button' is meaningful to its members, and the industrial typeface apparently reflects the church's space. Just fix the precise size of the secondary type—it should match either the width of 'WAREHOUSE' or the width of 'HOUSE.' Any other width is random."

Creative firm
Tomko Design
Phoenix, AZ

Client
Good Impressions

Industry
Printing

 "While the 'G' of 'GOOD' has been customized to reflect the logo, the 'G' of 'PRINTING' hasn't. Internal continuity in a logo is a good goal for which to strive."

 "Just enough customization and dimensionality to make it the client's own mark. 'PRINTING' looks wimpy: too light to carry the red color, too long to agree with 'GOOD,' and too short to agree with 'IMPRESSIONS.'"

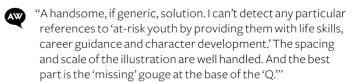

Creative firm
Rome & Gold Creative
Albuquerque, NM

Client
LifeQuest

Industry
At-Risk Youth Nonprofit Organization

 LifeQuest works with at-risk youth by providing life skills, career guidance, and character development.

Creative firm
Inertia Graphics
Hagerstown, MD

Client
GT Lawn Service

Industry
Lawn Service

RH "Without the explanation, I'd guess this logo is for fat people who sit on cushions."

AW "A handsome, if generic, solution. I can't detect any particular references to 'at-risk youth by providing them with life skills, career guidance and character development.' The spacing and scale of the illustration are well handled. And the best part is the 'missing' gouge at the base of the 'Q.'"

RH "A change in point size, color, and letterspacing is overdoing the complexity. Plus, it's generally best to avoid artificially stretching or condensing type—use an extended or condensed font instead."

AW "The stroke weight consistency unifies the illustration and the type. Given the shape of the other elements, diamonds would be a better choice than the round bullets."

Creative firm
Ariana Palacios Rivas
London, UK

Client
Tixmob

Industry
Mobile Ticketing Service

 "Many logos combine two familiar items to produce a hybrid—and this is a good example of why it can work so well. Descriptive and clear. Technically, the lines that are intended to resemble buttons on the phone don't sit in correct perspective, and so appear to be floating off the curved surface."

"An illustrated cell phone–ticket combination precisely describes the service this company provides. The missing stroke on the bold 'b' is perfectly excised, but I would want to see a parallel version in which the secondary type's 'b' in 'mobile' has the same treatment, just to be sure it doesn't, in fact, *need* the same treatment."

Creative firm
Brain Magnet
Saint Cloud, MN

Client
Cloud Cartographics

Industry
Mapping

 "I agree with Alex's detailed comments (below) about the sizes of the 'C' and 'O' in cloud. The lettering style is unique and appropriate for a client who deals with precision geometry. My only quibble about the mark is the transition from the cloud into the border. The curve feels suddenly too tight and should be resolved as either a softer curve or a point."

 "The illustration is without possible improvement. The type, though, has a couple of interesting issues. I will bet that these letters were drawn by the designer rather than found in a font. While the shapes are cut-and-paste geometry, the 'tells' are the width of the 'L' and the mathematically correct but visually too small 'C' and 'O' in 'CLOUD.'"

"The 'L' is way too wide in relation to its neighbors. All three letters got that way because they follow the same square-based grid. I always applaud self-created letterforms, because they help define a unique personality for the client."

249

Creative firm
Dustin Commer
Wichita, KS

Client
Dustin Commer

Industry
Animal Behaviorist

Creative firm
Wolken Communications
Seattle, WA

Client
Just Cauz

Industry
Philanthropy

Creative firm
Tomko Design
Phoenix, AZ

Client
Element Ozone

Industry
Water Purification

Creative firm
MINE
San Francisco, CA

Client
Golden Gate Helicopters

Industry
Tourism, Entertainment

RH "Dog plus healing hands—a well-executed logo successfully combining two elements. I did, however, originally read it as a dog with its eyes covered and so, at first, thought it was a logo for a guide-dogs-for-the-blind organization."

AW "Hands-on pet healing via the time clock–punching Looney Tunes sheepdog. First rate!"

MC "This logo is strong and impactful even at a small size. The colors and the simple sans serif work well for the stated target. The silhouettes don't stand up to scrutiny at larger sizes. The details need to be adjusted to make them feel more intentional and consistent."

RH "Using figures serves to personalize this logo and also make it relevant to its target market. The figures successfully represent the 20s to 40s age bracket to which this design, produced for a company focused on making donating money more accessible, is intended to appeal.

"The autotraced figures have lost some of their natural flow and detail—the hands in particular are less than convincing. Though the poses are convincing and characterful, using a silhouette derived directly from a photograph would have been better."

AW "Direct, clean mark for a philanthropy for people in their 20s to 40s. There is a peculiar left leg/right leg, smooth/wiggly treatment, and the feet look overly simplified and distorted. Whether or not this is an autotrace result, the illustration should be corrected by hand until all inadvertant oddities are removed."

RH "Using custom type is always a good way to create a unique logo, one that by definition will be different from the competition. Custom type design needs a rigorous understanding of letter construction.

"Here we have a good example of the straight-line-meets-curve problem. The semicircular elements of the 'm' and 'n' seem to have kinks where they meet the uprights. These need to be smoothed out.

"The alignment of the ascenders and the three-circle icon (a graphic representation of the ozone molecule O3), and the equivalence of space between all the elements is consistent and lends the mark refinement."

AW "Love the triad mark—perfect spacing and scale. The nearly closed 'e's are fine, but the extended horizontals of the 'z' become a second focal point, fighting with the ozone molecule for attention."

RH "Another monogram-derived design. This manages to be sleek and elegant, and the gold and red on cream color scheme definitely helps the perception of a luxury brand."

AW "'G's become faces in this handsome mark for a California helicopter service in which flight is abstractly merged with hair."

Creative firm
A3 Design
Charlotte, NC

Client
Carbonhouse

Industry
Creative

RH "The execution of the green leaf is very nicely echoed in the liquid inside the flask, complete with the white inline."

RM "This is a very well-executed logo. The curve of the leaf is a perfect arc to represent flowing water and it possesses great color combination that says 'environment and modern.'"

AW "'Greenhouse' is well centered between the secondary type and the illustration. If the flask were a bit larger, it would definitely be the focal point instead of being about equally important as 'greenhouse.'"

Creative firm
Roskelly, Inc.
Portsmouth, RI

Client
Guck Boats

Industry
Marine Manufacturing

RH "A simple idea—the shape of the company's product is the shape of the logo—but here very nicely executed. The execution of the 'G' is uncontrived and even has a keel."

AW "Very, very nicely handled. The details are all well attended to implying an equally well-made boat."

Creative firm
Timber Design Company
Indianapolis, IN

Client
Indiana Urban Forest Council

Industry
Urban Forestry

Creative firm
Type G Design
Carlsbad, CA

Client
Pasta Moto

Industry
Italian Restaurant Chain

 "This elongated shield logo has a simple color palette and easy-to-read type. The illustration says exactly enough in a well-crafted and direct way. The simplicity of the design should allow it to convert to an embroidered patch or silkscreened decal quite well."

RM "A great use of shapes helps tell the story of the organization. The tree knocked out with the solid tress in the foreground creates a perfect place to set the type."

AW "Layering silhouettes is a simple and sure way to create a handsome, simple mark. The slight curve in 'COUNCIL' implies a relationship with the leaf at the bottom, so the curve should be increased and the closeness of those two elements adjusted."

 "This is a great illustration that's rather lost below the visually dominant type. The arched arrangement of 'PASTA' with the extremely pointy-topped letters creates a rather unfortunate openness between the 'A' and 'S.' I would recommend either a different font or a more horizontal arrangement."

 "The primary type sure looks like Italian Art Deco, but royalties go to Vespa!"

Creative firm
Robison Creative Studios
Springfield, MO

Client
Superior Image

Industry
Printing

 "There are several nice things going on with this mark. The transition from solid outline to dots of graduating sizes is done with an eye for reproduction, and the asymmetry of the treatment lends visual interest—almost an optical illusion at small sizes. The simply handled type lets the monogram stand out."

 "Excellent letterform manipulation in the 'S.'"

Creative firm
Jacob Tyler Creative Group
San Diego, CA

Client
University Thongs

Industry
Retail

 "Not sure whether this is a logo for an apparel company or a team of guys with a rich fantasy life; either way it's an arresting mark. I don't think the thong really needs the slightly darker outline though; less is more in design, as well as lingerie."

 "'University Thongs'? The mind boggles. Great combination of type and image, however."

 "Bend the 'U' in just a tiny bit at the three stress points to add a subtle touch of realism."

Creative firm
Mytton Williams
Bath, UK

Client
Brightlines Translation

Industry
Communication Services

 "I like that they didn't try to do too much with a company that works in a complex field. The color seems too playful for dealing with international markets, but hopefully this differentiates them in a good way."

 "Sensitively sized and positioned. The resulting positive space—the blue 'B'—is one funky letterform reminiscent of the late-1960s."

Creative firm
Misha Birmele Designer Graphics
Pasadena, CA

Client
Freeze Frame

Industry
Film, Television, Media

 "The vertical bar introduces a barrier—it seems to freeze the reader's eye momentarily as it moves from left to right. This bar and the change in weight mean that a letterspace between the words is unneccessary and that readability is not impaired."

 "A basic shift in weight is a great way to break words, add interest, or give emphasis. This company's identity comes across in the smart use of an industry-recognized bar from a timeline to also break the words."

 "This mark makes the most of a simple vertical stroke as an illustrative element. That is smart."

Creative firm
Fauxkoi Design Company
Minneapolis, MN

Client
Catlick Records

Industry
Music

 "This feels like balloon animals reshaped into letters with an outer protective layer. It's fun and cute but has some technical problems.

"Since line weight is so important in a logo like this, all line weights should be looked at. I'm referring to the eye of the 'e.' Adjustments should be made to maintain the weight of the white line. More problems occur where the 'a' and 'p' return to almost touch."

Creative firm
Fauxkoi Design Company
Minneapolis, MN

Client
Heidi Munson Photography

Industry
Photography

 "I get a fun, whimsical, and almost daydream feeling from the cloud shapes, and I'm sure her young models enjoy that. But this heavy, sharp-edged type with solid counters really just puts a damper on the playfulness.

"Overall, the blue circles can be a great holding shape that can work with almost anything in any arrangements. That can give you a lot of options with the identity down the road."

 "Love the lowercase 'i's, but they create real spacing inconsistencies with 'munson,' which is much too tight. 'Photography' is randomly located but is acceptable in the context of random counter filling."

Creative firm
Fauxkoi Design Company
Minneapolis, MN

Client
Mill City Press

Industry
Online Self-Publishing

 "A design that harks back to the days of heavy industry—a nice twist, seeing as it's for an online publisher rather than a traditional press!"

 "Solid and established. The press may be brand new but you get a sense of history and experience. Some technical problems might be: the legs of the water tower and the stack under the 'Y.' They can be tricky since they don't really have an edge to line up with.

"Also, the vanishing point should have the stacks and large letters above be closer, not farther, from each other. Overall, this is an effective logo for conveying an established press."

Creative firm
Robison Creative Studios
Springfield, MO

Client
Zion Church

Industry
Religion

 "There's a dove hiding in that leaf… or is it a flame?"

 "The weight of the dove/flame negative space is carefully equalized to the weight of the three letterforms in this mark. And the letterspacing is even. Technically well done."

YogaStudio

YogaStudio

YogaStudio

YogaStudio

YogaStudio

Creative firm
Giotto
Quito, Ecuador

Client
Yoga Studio

Industry
Sports

RH "An interesting execution of the human form. Some of these shapes border on the completely abstract when seen in isolation, but as a group, the meaning is clear."

AW "Absolutely refreshing work. The thinness of the figures' strokes, which matches the lighter type, enhances the feeling of anti-gravity."

Creative firm
Espial
Johannesburg, South Africa

Client
University of the Witwatersrand

Industry
Education

 "Many patterns are combined with finesse to create this wonderfully detailed seal. The type around the circle is beautifully spaced. My only quibble is the descending 'J.' I would have shortened it so that it aligned with the baseline. As it is, my eye goes there first, and I find it a bit distracting from the other lovely elements."

 "Great central artwork. The choice of typeface is suspect, saying nothing at all about ancient heritage or South Africa. The diamond-shaped bullets look typeset when an interpretation of a more distinctive part of the illustration could have been applied. Lovely subtlety in the colors and tints."

Creative firm
3
Albuquerque, NM

Client
Albuquerque The Magazine

Industry
Publishing

 "This must be the first logo for a magazine that actually has a magazine illustration in the logo. One would think that adding 'THE MAGAZINE' as a tagline as well might be considered ramming home the point just a little too forcefully."

"The use of the two decenders on the 'q's' provides the symmetry for the open pages, completed by the wave-motif top and bottom, all executed in the same line width to give overall cohesion."

 "The critical touch is the way the bottoms of the 'q's' descenders are trimmed at angles so they can be seen equally as book parts and letterfoms."

CHRIS ENRIGHT | VOICEOVER ARTIST

Creative firm
Loop Design
Brooklyn, NY

Client
Chris Enright

Industry
Voice Work

 "A good use of a silhouette—the simple black treatment links it to the graphic elements (the type and the palette-as-speech balloon), yet the fact that it's derived from a photo gives it life and verisimilitude—appropriate for a service based on an individual's personality."

"The palette balloon effectively illustrates the range of tones of voice the artist can provide. The simple and restrained use of color is well judged—another designer might have been tempted to use color elsewhere—for example, in the text below. This would, of course, just have diluted the logo's conceptual strength."

 "A painter's palette as a speech bubble! The silhouetted figure's blackness relates the two elements. Still this looks like three elements in proximity, rather than a unified single mark, because they don't agree in very many ways beyond their blackness."

Creative firm
Jan Sabach Design
Munich, Germany

Client
Fresh Research

Industry
Marketing Research

 "A magnified image that doesn't show the magnifying glass but still communicates the idea. As a versatile symbol, the magnifying glass is a designer's favorite—it indicates looking closer, examining, revealing detail. Here it is pressed into use for a London-based company specializing in online marketing research."

 "Any abstracted letterform is a good letterform, especially if the character's essence is retained, as in this mark. The abstracted magnifying glass is implied by the curve and the enlarged half of the 'R.'"

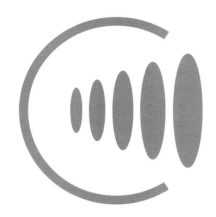

Creative firm
Jan Sabach Design
Munich, Germany

Client
Unilever

Industry
Marketing Research

Creative firm
Niedermeier Design
Seattle, WA

Client
Conversay

Industry
Voice Recognition

 "The foreground 'W' acts as a window through which the ornate script 'W' is visible. By combining two very different type forms successfully, the idea of the coming together of different styles—in this case an Internet-based community of female trendsetters—is effectively communicated."

 "This is a study in figure/ground relationship. The breezy 'W' doesn't actually exist: it is the leftover where pieces of the purple 'W' end. Our eyes recognize patterns that are familiar, so rather than seeing the six very peculiar purple shapes, we see a white script letter 'in front of' a chunky purple letter."

 "This logo for a voice recognition technology company, Conversay, presses the intital 'C' into double duty both as a monogram and as a mouth, speaking in a series of ellipses that indicate sound. The traditional depiction of sound is as a series of concentric curves, and I'd have liked to have seen that option explored here—the curves could have reflected the shape of the 'C.' Still, a simple and memorable mark."

 "The 'C' letterform has been abstracted into a speaker or a mouth. The spacing between the oval shapes—the sound— relates perfectly to the line width of the 'C,' unifying them."

Creative firm
The Decoder Ring
Austin, TX

Client
Otis Saves

Industry
Bar and Music Venue

 "Otis Saves is an unusual name for a bar and music venue…
but why not? The script and the surrounding circle are
beautifully balanced, and repeating the name in Futura
below counters any criticism about readability. Otis Saves…
but Sam Cooke scores on the rebound."

 "Wonderful contrast of script and geometric letterforms.
Breaking 'Otis' syllabically works because we read the two
parts in the correct order: the 'O' is bigger and bolder, the 'tis'
is smaller. Great work."

Creative firm
Transpire Design
Denver, CO

Client
Juntos Argentina

Industry
Non profit

 "Handsome form and intelligent, restrained use of color distinguish this excellent mark. The typeface is Trajan, whose
serifs could have been emulated in the way the hands taper
off to increase unity."

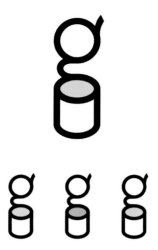

Creative firm
A3 Design
Charlotte, NC

Client
Goody's Paint Company

Industry
Home Decor

 "A clean, simple, monoline execution reminiscent of the work of Patrick Caulfield. I see a paint pot, but I also see a pedal bin…"

 "A 'g' and paint can combination uses a very simple geometrically-drawn letterform and very careful balance between the scale of the can and the counter space of the top of the 'g.' The use of primary colors is, to me, a bit banal."

Creative firm
Komprehensive Design
King of Prussia, PA

Client
Jeanne Komp

Industry
Educational Game

 "There's a bit too much unconvincing, distressed texture here, but the play on words is amusing. Is it guns at dawn if you break any typographic laws?"

 "All rules are meant to be broken, and this one manipulates the rule that all words must be spelled correctly. The flourishes are unneccessary: cover them to see the idea become clearer. The weathering effect and the type choice convey plenty of old west attitude. Then plunk some of that blue into the star, and the parts become a whole."

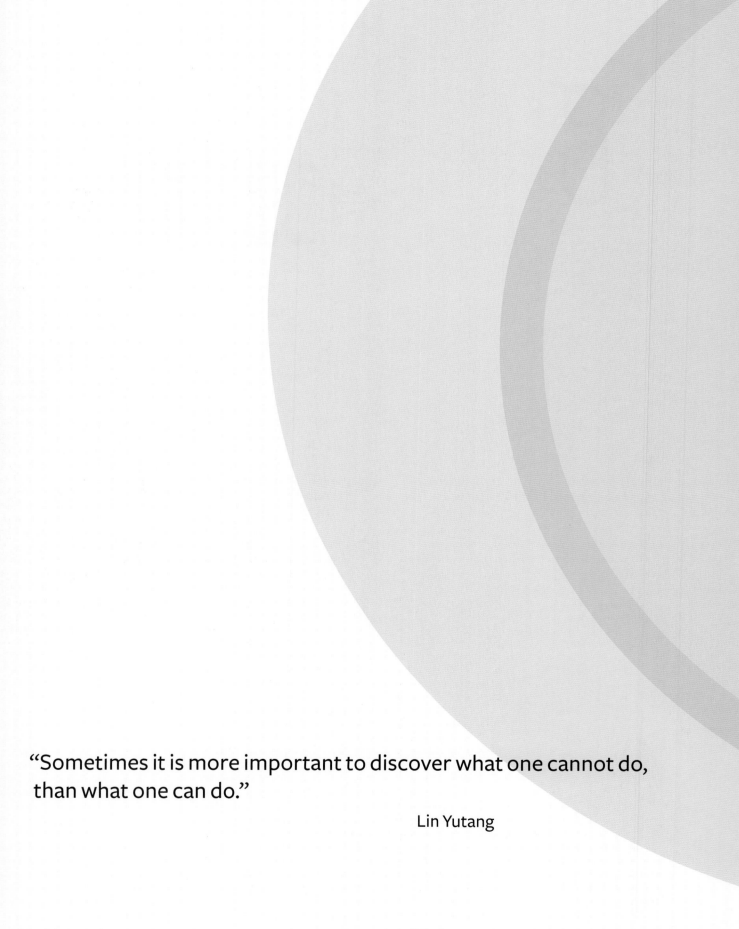

"Sometimes it is more important to discover what one cannot do, than what one can do."

Lin Yutang

BONUS CHAPTER
Not-So-Good Logos, Explained

THE **LUCY WALLIS** FOUNDATION

 "A logo is a microcosm of graphic design. There are a limited number of relationships that must be resolved in a way that looks thoughtful and purposeful. And a logo must have a balance of contrasts to make it visible and similarities to give it design unity.

"As in any other application of design principles, it is not enough to merely have 'nothing wrong' with a logo. There must be something demonstrably 'right' with a logo. So, what is good about this 'calligraphy,' (which means 'beautiful writing')? Is there a difference between good hand lettering and just some stuff? If so, what puts this in the first category? How does the underscore make any sense? One end is rounded; the other is chopped off.

"So this thing is really a collection of pieces that have nothing whatever to do with one another—with the lone exception that they are all black. That's a mighty thin layer of glue."

PHIL OSWALD
ORNITHOLOGIST

 "There is nothing memorable or unique about this mark. Without the type we would have no idea what it was about."

 "The font here was probably freeware or shareware, hence the lack of kerning. Look at the gappy 'SW' and 'ST' combinations. A designer with a good eye would have spotted these and corrected them manually. If your font is free, it's probably free for a reason. Use professionally designed fonts if you're a professional."

 "No concept, no cohesion, nothing to recommend it. Clients should not accept this level of design from a designer."

 "No, no, no—not with those bold initials."

RH "With an evocative name like 'SHIRTS FOR STUDS,' you'd think a little humor and an ounce of creativity would have been easy to come by. But no, we get a mess of bad letter-spacing, arbitrary color choices, and a collar that is so badly drawn it barely looks like a collar at all."

AW "Why are the 'S's blue? And the house (or shirt collar) shape is silly."

RH "Poor 'Bar and Grill' type choice. Three styles in one logo—western, radius-cornered grunge, and calligraphy."

RM "The proportions of these elements work when viewed small. But when you study the type forms and the execution—it falls apart. Something—some element—needs to carry the day and the rest becomes supporting cast. Instead we have a competing trio."

RH "Three current design trends arbitrarily thrown together without a unifying concept. Style over substance."

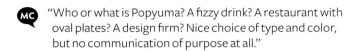

MC "Who or what is Popyuma? A fizzy drink? A restaurant with oval plates? A design firm? Nice choice of type and color, but no communication of purpose at all."

AW "What is 'right' about the positioning of these ovals? 'Popyuma' is so simple I am tempted to think the ovals are a conscious contrast, but they're not random enough to really appear to have been randomly placed."

MC "This is a great example of why you need hand lettering to make logos great. Although the Blackletter treatment here is extremely cliché, it could have at least been GOOD cliché if the designer had spent some time working out the relationships between the shapes by customizing the letter-forms instead of relying on a typeface. The swashes should interact and relate to the letters; these are just placed clip art. As it is, this is only a preliminary type arrangement, not a logo."

RH "Please, no more Blackletters on hip-hop albums. Cliché upon cliché. And get a phukkin dickshunry while you're at it. Not every other word ends in a 'z.' "

RM "I am sure a lot of thinking went into this logo and the addition of the ornament to the 'K.' I wish I knew what that thinking was."

AW "One of the most difficult design assignments is to create a mark for your own company. I do not recall having ever seen a flourish added to a bold sans serif before. It is so counter-intuitive that it startles."

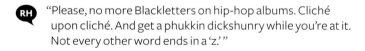

RH "Truly horrible. An object lesson in why mastery of Photoshop and type-bending tools does not make you a graphic designer. And why visually tone-deaf clients, who accept and pay for this rubbish, put good designers out of business.

"Horrible clashing colors, drop shadows—blurred and non-blurred mixed, amateur ligatures and noncentered 'X,' arbitrarily touching 'S' and 'X,' hideous use of grads, a ribbon—please, no."

RM "I hope the illustration represents the spine *before* seeing this chiropractor. A bit more thought should have gone into this one."

AW "Referencing medical illustration without actually being one, this mark says 'scientific' and 'spine.' Hermann Zapf's Palatino typeface has been expanded in 'BUNBURY,' presumably to better balance the two words. Sadly, the letterspacing in 'CHIROPRACTIC' has been reduced (for the same reason?), jamming the elegant letterforms together.

"Tweaking type is what we designers should do to manage the overall impression, but making type tweaks apparent is going too far. Our tricks should not be noticeable."

RH "There are some strange things happening here with the line spacing—it seems that 'PERSONAL & CONFIDENTIAL' is more related to 'SOLUTIONS' than 'SOLUTIONS' is related to 'FINANCIAL.' Just as type size is used to create a hierarchy, so is spacing, and here the proximity of certain elements works against the intended reading."

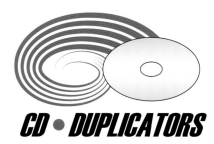

CD • DUPLICATORS

 "If the intention here was to create a brand that shouted 'cheap and nasty,' the designer has succeeded—in spades. A CD is probably one of the only good places to use a rainbow grad—and here we have an insipid blue instead. Surely the sheer ugliness of this logo demands a rainbow grad, too?"

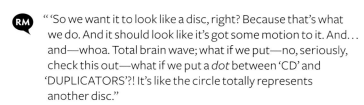 "'So we want it to look like a disc, right? Because that's what we do. And it should look like it's got some motion to it. And... and—whoa. Total brain wave; what if we put—no, seriously, check this out—what if we put a *dot* between 'CD' and 'DUPLICATORS'?! It's like the circle totally represents another disc."

discovery ⊿one

MC "There's a lot going on here. The arrow and eye feel like pickup clip art that's been added to some swirls. Aside from being overused, they don't seem to relate well to the background shapes or the type. Simplification would help the communication."

AW "Elegance in design is defined as the absence of complexity. There is a lot of contrast that can be removed from this mark to approach elegance. The arrow and eye are stock icons that do not go together stylistically. The lowercase 'discovery' should be all caps to go with the lining figured 'zone.' And the 'c-e'-triangle has too many shapes and colors for unity: let the negative space shapes do more of the work."

LAUNDRY DETERGENT

RH "'KLEEN NOW' is obviously powerful—half the 'K' has been wiped off already!"

AW "'LAUNDRY DETERGENT' is unresolved, so it makes the mark look busy. It contrasts by size, typeface, color, position, and line spacing (which is much greater than between 'KLEEN' and 'NOW'). It is similar by proximity and horizontal baseline. That's not enough for design unity."

RH "Outlines, drop shadows, lozenges—wahoo! Let's see what this other tool in Illustrator does and pile that in, too. 'MACK' isn't even centered vertically in the orange lozenge, which is tellingly slipshod."

AW "Space is properly used when fences are unnecessary. These shapes all have black perimeters, and that breaks up a single entity into four stacked pieces. 'FLORIST' should be bigger to absorb that weakening letterspacing, and on a darker background or, like 'MACK,' outlined in red to increase its status."

RH "It's the old folded corner idea! I'll bet every art student's tried this at least once. Leave it at college where it belongs. At least here it doubles as a forward-pointing arrow, but in doing double duty now it doesn't look correct as a folded corner."

AW "The bent corner should be better integrated with the letterforms so the two elements become one. The rounded corners couldn't be less purposefully contrasting, though they are better handled than the angular top right corner."

RH "There is a stylistic mismatch between the curves of the image and the angularity of the type. Though purposeful tension can be a good thing, it sometimes can seem as if the logo is made from two different concepts bolted together."

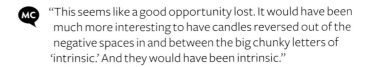

"This seems like a good opportunity lost. It would have been much more interesting to have candles reversed out of the negative spaces in and between the big chunky letters of 'intrinsic.' And they would have been intrinsic."

"Why is one candle yellow? Why is the Futura 'CANDLES' not ranged to the same width? Why the two fonts in the first place? Why... did the designer bother?"

"A change in font, letterspacing, AND size is overdoing matters—it would be more simple and elegant to change just one, for emphasis. The Palatino is crash-kerned, while the Futura is too thin, too widely spaced, and too close to the Palatino. When your line spacing (leading) is smaller than your word spacing, problems of balance and legibility will occur."

"Three unrelated elements placed near one another. This is not enough to be a logo. At least use the same geometric 'C' in both the illustration and in 'Craft.'"

"Uninspired and literal. Autotraced photographs can have the stylistic signature of the computer program laying far too heavily on them."

 "This feels very 'me too.' I like Jonathan Adler colors, but beyond that, I don't get a feeling these guys are doing anything original. This could be a logo for anything from furniture to hair care."

 "Nice colors; dull execution."

 "Pangea yogurt was established to provide a new kind of yogurt marketed to a younger demographic. To achieve this here, the designer has used 'club flyer' style type. While marketing to a specific target audience makes this kind of choice of letterforms seem sensible, crossing a techno font with a food product will look just silly in five years when club fashions have moved on—like lowriders on your bank manager.

"Good solutions come from the inside out, not the outside in. The first is designing from solid principles derived from the product, be it a rock band, novel, or toothpaste. The second is not design at all; it's marketing—making something resemble something else to grab a perceived audience. This is why 'own brand' products often look very much like other leading brands. If the intention is to attract a new audience, it's possible to design an original yogurt logo that looks modern and youthful without inappropriate borrowing. Truly dire letterspacing and an arbitrary flourish just dig the hole deeper."

SUSAN GRACE HILLS
EVENT PLANNER

 "Love the green 'S's, but not too keen on the last enlarged 'S' of 'HillS' because it is the single strangest element of this design. As such, it competes with the things that are worthy of being noticed, like that odd—but fun—little white curve. The typeface has no formal relationship to these 'S' curves."

 "Cliché ideas can often work well to communicate because they ARE cliché—everyone understands them. If you're going to rely on a cliché, however, you must put some work into the design to make it unique and differentiating.

"This logo could have been interesting if the forms and weights were handled in a less conventional way. This execution lacks any uniqueness and will never make a strong or memorable impression. Two good examples of arrows used well are the FedEx and Burton logos in the 'Author Favorites' chapter."

 "Arrows pointing up and to the right, as used here, are a common motif used to denote success and forward movement, probably due to the resemblance to a graph. However, it is an overused and somewhat generic concept."

PUREFOY
bakery

 "A change in point size, color, and letterspacing is overdoing the complexity. Plus, it's generaly best to avoid artificially stretching or condensing type. Use an extended or condensed font instead."

MC "This is a nice idea that should have been sent to a calligrapher or a better hand-letterer for refinement. The script here is extremely awkward and lumpy looking with a hugely out-of-scale ampersand and a weak initial 'W,' to name only a few of its many flaws."

RH "This logo falls between two stools—neither 'custom' and handmade enough, nor refined and polished enough, but a bit of both awkwardly combined. Willem and Strom Custom Carpentry is a Memphis, Tennessee–based company that specializes in custom woodworking such as kitchen cabinetry, tables, entertainment centers, and bathrooms, so a logo that spoke of hand-finished artistry would be an entirely appropriate solution. This, unfortunately, with its awkward swashes and grad rules, isn't it."

RM "At first glance, this type treatment looks very elegant, but upon a closer look, it is not legible and feels unfinished."

MC "This is yet another logo using a tree, so we're not giving any points for originality. That leaves execution, and I can't give this one many kudos there either. The tree itself feels like an awkwardly streamlined blob with an unrelated house knocked out of it. The type is uninspired."

RH "A limply drawn tree that looks like a poor autotrace and a stylized house make for a cliché-ridden logo."

"Who's gonna dare to be great?"

Muhammad Ali

JUST FOR FUN
Author Favorites, Explained

MC "The Apple logo has become one of the most ubiquitous icons in most designers' lives. I love it both for its inherent simplicity and for the restraint and consistency with which it is applied. Entering the Apple store is like entering the church of design—it makes me very happy!"

MC "The colorful NBC peacock is a classic. Chermayeff and Geismar's update is timeless, simple, and elegant."

AW "This logo is so good that NBC returned to it after a few years of misadventure with their red and blue 'N' mark."

MC "Who doesn't love the bunny in a bow tie? This is another great example of 'less is more' when it comes to great icon design."

CREDITS:
Apple, Inc.   Creative firm: Regis McKenna   Industry: Computers & Consumer Electronics
NBC   Creative firm: Chermayeff & Geismar Associates   Industry: Broadcasting
PEI, Inc.   Designer: Arthur Paul   Industry: Publishing

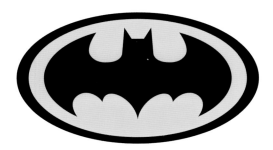

"I love this panda icon for its wonderful use of negative space and the expression on his face. Leaving out the eyes makes him seem a bit sad, an expression that inspires sympathy and probably makes him a fabulous fund-raiser."

"I love this emblem of one of DC's iconic heroes, Batman. The 1989 movie poster didn't need anything else."

"Simplicity and purity last forever."

"The recent Burton Snowboards logo is a lowercase 'b' formed by a curved arrow, like a good carved turn. It's clean and classic and looks great on gear. I wish I'd done it."

CREDITS:
World Wildlife Fund   Creative firm: Landor Associates   Industry: Nonprofit
Batman   Designer: Bob Kane   Industry: Publishing, Entertainment
Burton   Creative firm: JDK Design   Industry: Sporting Goods

CHANEL

adidas

 "I can't decide whether I like the Chanel lettering or the monogram more. They're both so classic that it's hard to separate them. They were perfectly modern when they were created and over the years they've never felt outdated. This is a perfect example of timeless design."

 "This icon is hard to separate from the apparel it usually adorns. It's a great example of reviving a period icon and making something old, new again."

"The 'Three Stripes' was a brand and a shoe-identifying decoration long before Nike came along."

ABSOLUT®
Country of Sweden
VODKA

 "I love the lettering on the Absolute bottle. The brand uses the bold type without the script in many applications, but I think it loses something key without the script. The tension between the styles really creates a statement of strength and elegance combined."

CREDITS:
Chanel Designer: Unknown   Industry: Cosmetics
Adidas Designer: Peter Moore   Industry: Sportswear
Absolut Vodka Designer: Unknown   Industry: Beverages

 "Like the FedEx logo, this one has a great hidden symbol. The face is also a lowercase 'g.' That gift of a letter was taken skillful advantage of to create a logo that makes everyone feel good about getting rid of their old stuff!"

"On Oct. 17, 1951, CBS unveiled its new logo, the CBS Eye, which is one of the best-crafted, most identifiable, and most successful corporate symbols in history. If there are any designers out there who don't know and love this icon, they need to go back for some remedial design history work."

"Invented at the dawn of television and the visual age, this mark is simply brilliant in its stylized illustration. The balance of figure and ground is perfectly realized."

 "This penguin has gone though a lot of changes over time, but in spite of the multiple positions, he's never lost his basic identity."

CREDITS:
Goodwill   Designer: Joseph Selame   Industry: Nonprofit
CBS   Designer: William Golden   Industry: Broadcasting
Penguin   Designer: Jan Tschichold   Industry: Publishing

 "The Harley shield has been updated, but it's never been redesigned. It's a classic example of a company that honors its roots. The lettering fits beautifully into the shield and bar, and the company uses it so consistently and respectfully that it's one of those logos I can recognize easily—even at 80 mph."

 "When this logo first came out, it was accompanied by ads that animated the green leaves or turned it into a sun. Its beautiful shapes and colors created a whole new way of thinking about petroleum—just what was intended, I'm sure."

 "The New Haven Railroad logo by Herbert Matter, 1954, features precise management of white space."

CREDITS:
Harley-Davidson   Creative firm: Unknown   Industry: Motorcycles
British Petroleum   Creative firm: Landor Associates   Industry: Oil
New Haven Railroad   Designer: Herbert Matter   Industry: Locomotive

RM "The last generation Northwest Airlines logo. Every time I look at it, I feel the joy the designer must have felt when he discovered that the triangle pointing to the northwest also completed the 'W' in such a simple and meaningful way."

AW "The Northwest Airlines logo by Landor Associates, 1990. Getting two letters, 'N' and 'W,' and a diagram to blend perfectly is brilliant. The updated logo, introduced in 2003, retains only the logo's diagrammatic meaning."

RH "The S. H. A. D. O. uniform logo from the British television series *UFO* is pretty clunky, but it was one of the first instances where I realized there was such a thing as logo design. I cut a copy of the logo out of a bubblegum card, taped a safety pin to the back, and wore it to school.

"S. H. A. D. O. stands for Supreme Headquarters Alien Defence Organization, of course."

MC "I love the FedEx logo. The arrow in the negative space is a great visual test. Lots of people don't notice it."

CREDITS:
Northwest Airlines Creative firm: Landor Associates   Industry: Airline
S.H.A.D.O. Designer: Unknown   Industry: Entertainment
FedEx Creative firm: Landor Associates   Industry: Courier

 "I've always like the bent-staple 'L' in this logo. It includes just enough information to be memorable and understood and nothing more."

"The Olympic rings logo, originally drawn in 1913 by Pierre de Frédy, Baron de Coubertin, the founder of the modern Olympic Games. It was redrawn by Otl Aicher as part of his brilliant 1972 Munich Games icon set."

"Hot Wheels—it's a logo made from flames! It sounds like it shouldn't work, and yet it does. This again is a design from a simpler age, when logos did what they said on the tin. It's been tweaked over the years with the additions of Photoshop meddling and detail, but at heart it's still the same design. A winner."

CREDITS:
Staples Designer: Unknown Industry: Office Supplies
International Olympics Designer: Baron Pierre de Coubertin Industry: Professional Sports
Hot Wheels Designer: Rick Irons Industry: Toys

AW "Mighty simplistic, but there is nothing that can or should be changed. It is timeless in its modernism."

RH "The reason I like this logo is its sense of humor, it's noncorporate friendliness, and it's immediate 'recognizability.' It comes from a simpler age of design when logos were not pared down to the bare essentials and so has the quirkiness and character that have been ironed out of many modern logos. Classic."

AW "What wonderful custom lettering that emphasizes the 'frozen sound' nature of typography. Suuuuuuuuuuupima."

CREDITS:
YLighting Designer: Mattison for YLighting   Industry: Lighting
Michelin Designer: Unknown   Industry: Automotive
Supima Designer: Unknown   Industry: Textile

 "The Cingular logo is cheerful, simple, and fun. I'm sorry AT&T has discontinued the Cingular brand. I'll miss the little guy."

 "Two heavy Helvetica characters jammed against each other. The 3M logo has shown a way for a new generation of designers to rescue Miedinger's classic modernist font from corporate conformity and reappropriate it for more cutting-edge uses."

 "After Chanel, this is my favorite type-only logo of all time. Fabien Baron is a master typographer and it really shows in the simplicity and elegance of these four letters."

CREDITS:
Cingular   Designer: Jamie Koval at VSA Partners   Industry: Telecommunications
3M   Designer: Siegal & Gale   Industry: Industrial Technology
NARS Cosmetics   Designer: Fabien Baron   Industry: Cosmetics

INDEX